SPIRITUALITY
IN SOCIAL WORK PRACTICE

Narratives for Professional Helping

Edited by Sonia Leib Abels
Founding Editor, REFLECTIONS

LOVE PUBLISHIN
Denver • Londo

Published by Love Publishing Company
Denver, Colorado 80237

Printed in the U.S.A.
ISBN 0-89108-280-8
Library of Congress Catalog Card Number 00-130451

Contents

Preface

Inherent in the role of social workers and other professional helpers is to engage in thoughtful reflection on their experiences with the people they serve. This book examines spiritual facets of the practice of social work through a collection of narratives. These accounts were written by social workers in the true narrative style. They are personal stories revealing their experiences in practice and the meaning they gained from those experiences. The authors reflect on the spiritual components of their interactions, as well as their clients' spirituality.

Lending depth and breadth to these experiences are the rich diversity and cultural influences that people bring to their interactions with social workers. The narratives in this book cover the spiritual spectrum from Bedouin-Arab, to Kwanzaa, Christian, American Indian, Buddhist, and others. Concluding each narrative are questions that will aid readers in gaining insights into the meaning and significance of the narratives for themselves.

We hope the readers of this book will approach the narratives with a sense of reflection on themselves and the world. In doing so, this book can enrich the experiences of social workers and, in turn, the people they serve.

Sonia L. Abels
January, 2000

Contributors

● Meet The Editor

Sonia L. Abels is the Founding Editor of *Reflections: Narratives of Professional Helping.* This journal published by the Department of Social Work at California State University, Long Beach provides personal accounts of social work practice. She has served on the faculty at several universities in the United States and Europe.

● Meet The Contributors

Alean Al-Krenawi, Ph.D., Lecturer, Department of Social Work, Ben-Gurion University of the Negev, Israel.

Dr. Maulana Karenga is professor and chair of the Department of Black Studies, California State University, Long Beach and creator of the African American holiday of Kwanzaa.

Sarah Sloan Kreutziger, DSW, ACSW, is Assistant Professor and Director of Continuing Education, School of Social Work, Tulane University, New Orleans, LA.

Sadye L. Logan, DSW, ACSW is I. DeQuincey Newman Professor, School of Social Work, University of South Carolina Columbia, SC.

Christine T. Lowery, Ph.D., Assistant Professor, School of Social Welfare, University of Wisconsin-Milwaukee, Milwaukee, WI.

Michael J. Sheridan, Ph.D. is Associate Professor, School of Social Work, Virginia Commonwealth University.

Arthur Soissons-Segal, Ph.D. is coordinator of Psycho-Social Rehabilitation, Hollywood Mental Health Center, Hollywood, CA.

Michael James Yellow Bird, is Assistant Professor, School of Social Welfare, University of Kansas. He received his Ph.D. from the University of Wisconsin-Madison.

Introduction

by Sonia Leib Abels

"In the millennium the tools will change but the artistic skills of storytelling will endure," said Mary Schmidt Campbell, Dean of the Tisch School of Arts at New York State University, responding to the *NY Times Magazine* editor about the special edition for the millennium.

Revelations of experience, constructed into narratives, is the classic genre for sharing human experience. Examining social work practice through nonfiction personal narratives bring the reader to closer involvement with the worker's effort, the lived concerns expressed by clients, and the world view of both. Philosopher Martha Nussbaum uses narratives in her law school classes at the University of Chicago, because it ". . . helps the reader imagine what it is like to live the life of another person who might, given changes in circumstances, be oneself or one of one's loved ones." The narrative style, ". . . promote(s) identification and sympathy in the reader. . . . this is especially so if they show the effect of circumstances on the emotions and the inner world." (Nussbaum p. 5)

Spirituality, the first theme in our narrative series, reflects workers' experiences and approaches to spirituality. We hope the narratives in this series serve to stimulate the reader to consider and compare his/her own practice experiences. The narrative metaphor is a path by which we can link others' stories with our own, and better understand our practice. The spirituality narratives, rich with passion, excitement, and sometimes disappointment, reveal the social worker's struggle to find the right outcome against the forces of happenstance on well-planned interventions. Narratives connect people; they are steeped with mystery, life's tension and drama. Tables, statistical accounts and analysis, albeit necessary, primarily provide information. Narratives have the capacity to aid us to see one another as fully human. For instance, findings on the success/failure of permanency planning is essential information for social workers, but erects only the shell. It does not provide the means to imagine what the child, parent, or social worker thought or felt, or what meaning these experiences had, nor adds an understanding of what to do differently as a result of the findings. The moral imperative is within the story. Abstract articles tend to draw implications of the content. Narratives allow the reader to draw his or her own meaning.

Practice narratives are literary records, presenting participants' voices in the process of change at various system levels. They are stories of social human beings, choosing, acting on decisions, and coping with the consequences. They're disturbing, raising in context, powerful emotions and reactions to the scenes that unfold, under girded by revelations of the inner feelings of the social worker struggling to make meaning of the encounter. Both successes and failures of social work practice illustrate the truth of the material presented, and point to the humanity of all participants in the process.

● Beginnings: Genesis

Selecting "Spirituality" as the first of the series is a synergistic irony. Asimov notes that Genesis literally means "coming into being." He implies a form of transformation explicated through story. (Asimov, 1968, p. 17). Words to describe spirituality are difficult to find without a poetic temper. With words, space is changed and filled; and spirituality becomes material.

What is spirituality?

Spirituality and religion are different and the same. Religion frequently is considered formalized practice (Siporin, 1986, Canda, 1988). Religious spirituality locates with G-D, or God and Jesus, or God and Mohammed, or Buddha, as the center. The practice of secular or non-religious spirituality may be considered a concept separate and apart from religious endeavors. Generally, it's considered "a set of personal beliefs derived from the individualistic perception of self and his or her relationship to both the natural world and the metaphysical realm." Spirituality, as does religion, has to do with meaning, purpose, and morality in a social context.

In a lead article in the *NY Times* (DeParle, p. A1) we meet a public welfare case worker, Mr. Steinborn, commenting on his work with his clients whose experiences move him deeply.

"I never wanted to be a sucker for a sob story. There's a lot of sadness and depression in the people I deal with. . . . They don't want to be perceived as vulnerable. But when you cut away the exterior, they're sad—sad for themselves, sad for their children, sad that they haven't done more with their lives. And they're just aching for you to listen—not necessarily to solve their problems, just to listen. I'm not sure if I learned this before and chose to forget it, or I'm learning for the first time."

Meditation is a form of spirituality, lighting candles for the Sabbath is spirituality, giving to the homeless could be a form of spirituality, going to church or the mosque is spiritual. Private or public prayer is spirituality. The creation of Kawanzaa was a spiritual act. I think spirituality means beyond the self: it is mindfulness, connectedness and community. While readers are invited to consider the meaning of spirituality for themselves, and its value for people they serve, teach and learn from, some other views may be helpful.

(The following views are taken from:
http://spiritual growth.com/spirituality/index.html p. 1–4)

● John Shea, a contemporary Catholic theologian says, "It is all of life." Ed Canda, a social work academic, and editor of the *Reflection's* issue "Spirituality" noted, "Spiritual development is not possible without careful reflection on the nature of oneself and the world." (1995) Vol. 1 #4. Alan Jones, Dean of Grace Cathedral, in San Francisco defined it as, "The are of making connections." David Ariel, a Rabbi, calls it "Heart Knowledge." Catholic Bishop Pedro Casidaliga, poet of the Amazon Indians said, "spirituality is a measure of our humanity . . ." Albert Einstein spoke of that "cosmic religious feeling." Barbara McClintock, the geneticist, ignored by her male colleagues and recognized by a Nobel prize, described it as a feeling of the organism; and "Spirituality is rooted in desire. We long for something we can neither name nor describe, but which is no less real because of our inability to capture it with words."

● Meaning for Social Work

In the past 15 years, spirituality in social work has reemerged from the late 19th century friendly visitors' (social workers) attempts to "save persons from sloth and indulgence." While the friendly visitor may have represented conservative economics, an upper class lifestyle, and social Darwinism, their spirituality came from Christian love and worthy intentions. (Dhuff, F.).

I consider spirituality to be a belief in the search for social justice, the desire to further the practice of respect for all persons. Respect means equality, autonomy, privacy and human development. We might say respect for persons is social work in action. It also could be said that spirituality is social work in action.

● References

Rosenthal, J. (1999). Letter from the editor, *New York Times Magazine,* Dec. 6, p. 35.

Nussbaum, M. (1995) *Poetic justice.* Boston: Beacon Press.

Asimov, I. (1968). *Asimov's guide to the Bible.* New York Random House.

deParle, J. (1999). For caseworker helping is a frustrating struggle. *NY Times,* December 10, p. 1A.

Canda, E. (1988). Conceptualizing spirituality for social work. *Social Thought* (Winter), 30–46.

Siporin, M. (1986). Contributions of religious values to social work and the law. *Social Thought* (Fall No. 3).

Canda, E. Spirituality, *Reflections* (1995), 1 (4).

http://spiritual growth.com/spirituality/index.html p. 1–4

Dhuff, F., *http/www.idbsy.edu/socwork/dhuff/history/chpts/1–4*

Reconciling Western Treatment and Traditional Healing: A Social Worker Walks with the Wind

by Alean Al-Krenawi, Ph.D.

This chapter shows how the first Bedouin-Arab clinical social worker in Israel deals with a Bedouin-Arab clientele in the Negev. Efforts to apply Western techniques created barriers to treating their mental health problems. The author recommends practitioners who work with traditional ethnic groups be culturally sensitive and accept their clients' use of traditional healing, and shows the overlap of traditional with modern healing.

In the last two decades, helping professionals have come to appreciate the importance of "cultural sensitivity," that is, of respecting and taking into consideration the specific culture of their clients in the design, planning and implementation of their interventions (Al-Krenawi & Graham, 1996; Burgest, 1982; Devore & Schlesinger, 1991; Green, 1982; Lum, 1982; Ragab, 1990). Yet practice remains harder than preaching, especially when deeply rooted Western practices come into contact with equally or more deeply rooted non-Western ways.

This chapter recounts the gradual reawakening of the author, a Western-trained Bedouin-Arab clinical social worker, to the culture of his people and his struggle to find a satisfactory way of helping his largely Bedouin-Arab clientele in the Negev region of Israel. Having

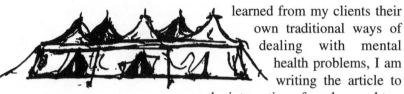

learned from my clients their own traditional ways of dealing with mental health problems, I am writing the article to urge the integration of modern and traditional modes of healing and to suggest ways of bridging the gap between "modern" clinicians and their "traditional" clients.

Similar points have been made by other writers on cross-cultural therapy, and I myself have made them elsewhere in more academic form. In this chapter, I have chosen to make them by telling about my own experiences in the hope that the account of the personal and professional dilemmas I faced as a Western-trained social worker, and of the ways in which I gradually resolved them, will give the reader a more tangible and sympathetic understanding both of the professional journey that is required to bridge the gap and of the traditional people whom we can help.

Before embarking on my personal account, I think it will be useful to provide a brief overview of the Bedouin-Arab of the Negev.

● The Bedouin-Arab of the Negev

The Bedouin-Arabs are a traditionally nomadic and tribal people who have inhabited many areas that are now in countries of northern Africa, the Arabian peninsula, and the Middle East (*Hebrew Encyclopedia*, 1954). Bedouin-Arabs have lived in the Middle East since before either Islam or Christianity became established religions. Among other places, they inhabited the Negev Desert. There are currently about 20 Bedouin-Arab tribes in the Negev, with a total of about 100,000 people. Forty percent live in villages, and 60 percent in clusters outside the villages (Al-Krenawi & Graham, 1997). Traditionally, Bedouin-Arabs have been nomads, earning their living by raising cattle, goats, and sheep. In the last 25 years, a rapid and dramatic process of urbanization has occurred, with increasing numbers of Bedouin-Arabs settling in villages and working in industry or services (Al-Krenawi & Graham, 1996).

Yet although this process has been accompanied by major cultural and social upheavals, Bedouin-Arab society is still anchored in its traditional ways. Like other traditional peoples, Bedouin-Arabs have a high context social structure, marked by a relatively slow pace of societal change, a high sense of social stability, and an emphasis on the collective over the individual (Al-Krenawi & Graham, 1997; Hall, 1976). In many essential ways, the society and culture of the Bedouin-Arabs of the Negev are still much like that of other traditional Arabs.

The core of the Arab—and Bedouin-Arab—social structure is the family. There are four main concentric family units. The largest is the tribe. Each tribe is headed by its own sheik and made up of several hamula. The hamula is the kinship group extending to a wide network of blood relations. Tribal decisions are made by forums of male elders representing the hamula (Abu-Khusa, 1994; Marks, 1974). Each hamula consists of the extended family, made up of parents, siblings, and their spouses and children. The smallest unit is the nuclear family—the married couple and their children (Al-Haj, 1989). The family is crucial to the homologous relationship between the individual and the group. To a considerable extent, social status, safety from economic hardship, and opportunity for personal development continue to rest on tribal and family identity.

Bedouin-Arab society is patriarchal, with men exercising the authority in the household, economy, and polity (Al-Krenawi & Graham, 1996). Polygamy is common practice, even among the well-educated and young (Al-Issa, 1990; Chaleby 1987; Chamie, 1986). Women's social status is strongly contingent on being married and rearing children, especially boys (Al-Sadawi, 1977). Bedouin-Arab women rarely leave the home unescorted, spend most of their time caring for the family, and generally still do not work outside the home (Al-Krenawi et al, 1994; Mass & Al-Krenawi, 1994).

The relation between the individual and family in Bedouin-Arab society is different from that in Western society. In Western families, children are expected to separate psychosocially from their parents and form their own autonomous identity (Erikson, 1963; Mahler, 1968). In Arab society, as in the traditional societies of Africa, Asia, South America, and the Middle East, the individual is expected to remain embedded in the collective family identity (Hofstede, 1989; Sue & Sue, 1990). Individuals live in a symbiotic relationship with their families, seeing themselves as extensions of a collective core identity. A family member who attempts to assert his/her own individuality will be condemned as deviant.

The development of modern therapy in Europe and North America was an extension of the development of Western individualism, nurtured by the climate of democracy. In Western therapy, as in Western society, the individual is viewed as an independent entity whose needs, rights, opinions, and values are to be respected and whose "self-actualization" is considered a worthy and important goal (Fromm, 1976; Pedersen et al, 1989). The clinician working with Bedouin-Arabs, on the other hand, must treat the client in the framework of his or her family.

● Traditional Mental Health Healers Among the Bedouin-Arab of the Negev

Among the traditions that the Bedouin-Arabs of the Negev still keep is that of the healer. The traditional Bedouin-Arab view of mental illness is that it comes from outside through sorcery, the evil eye, or evil spirits. Any of four types of traditional mental health healers may be consulted to counter the magic or expel the evil spirit:

1. The *Khatib* or *Hajjab* are male healers who produce amulets that are worn on the body to ward off evil spirits. This tradition is usually passed down from father to son, provided the latter is perceived as having sufficient literacy and community acceptance.

2. The *Dervish* treat mental illness using a variety of religious and cultural rituals. Both males and females can become *Dervishes* by receiving a *baraka* (or a blessing) from God, which is endorsed by a recognized Dervish.

3. The *Moalj Bel Koran,* or Koranic healer, works on the basis of religious principles derived from the Koran and treats patients who have been attacked by evil spirits. All Moalj Bel Koran are men, and most have some form of post-secondary education (Al-Krenawi & Graham, 1996). Koranic healing has gained popularity recently with the revival of Islam throughout the Muslim world.

4. The *Al-Fataha* is a fortune teller, who is usually consulted about psychosocial problems and who uses coffee grains to reveal any secret the patient may have. The role is usually passed down from mother to daughter (Al-Krenawi, 1995a; Al-Krenawi et al, 1995b).

Because of the structure of Bedouin-Arab society, an individual's illness, whether physical or mental, is considered the problem of the whole family, and the process of help seeking is a collaborative one in which the person's nuclear family, and sometimes the extended family as well, all take part. In response to the rapid social changes that Bedouin-Arab society of the Negev is undergoing, many families concurrently consult both modern practitioners and traditional healers (Al-Krenawi, 1995a, 1995b). While the GP at the local health fund clinic will refer the person to a social worker or psychiatrist, his or her family will also bring him or her to a traditional healer. Usually it is the woman of the house who encourages the visit to the tradi-

tional healer (Al-Issa, 1990; Al-Krenawi, 1995a; Koss-Chioino, 1992).

A 1974 study found that 70% of an examined population of Bedouin-Arab patients in Israel utilized traditional healers in tandem with modern treatment (Ben-Asa, 1974). The author's own study in the early 90's found that a good portion of his study population was still doing so (Al-Krenawi, 1992). Moreover, recent findings in various settings have shown that a combination of modern medicine and traditional healing can be quite effective in remedying mental health problems (Bokan & Campbell, 1984; Edwards, 1986; Jilek, 1994; Lambo, 1978; Lefley, 1986; New, 1977; Ruiz & Langrod, 1976a; Yoder, 1982).

Nonetheless, most Western-oriented professionals still give traditional healing short shrift, even when working with people who believe in it and who find the Western approach to mental health alien is not entirely helpful (Ruiz & Langrod, 1976b). This article is aimed at rectifying the bias.

● Walking With the Wind

I was born and raised in what is by Western standards a "traditional" culture. There are no documents indicating how long my family has lived in the Negev, but oral tradition places it at several hundred years.

My grandparents, like their forebears, were nomads. My parents became semi-nomadic only in my early childhood. Living in a tent close to the other 2,000 or so members of the tribe, we led tribal lives. My cousins, grandparents, aunts and uncles, and other members of the tribe all exerted considerable influence on our daily doings. As a child, I was familiar with the various kinds of traditional healers. My grandfather, with whom I lived for several years, was an amulet writer, one of the four types of traditional healers I wrote about above. I used to serve his clients coffee and tea as they waited to see him. When the treatment was carried out in front of everyone, as it often was, I watched. I often chatted with the clients and my grandfather was happy to answer my many questions.

The third of fifteen children, I was blessed with the chance to get an education. I rode a donkey 10 kilometers to school, returned home every day to tend sheep, and carried water from a well to our home. For high school, I attended a boarding school in an Arab village in the center of Israel, far from home. This was the first time in my life that I was among well educated Arabs. Since I did well in my studies and received a good deal of encouragement from my teachers, I gradually came to see myself as part of this world, the educated world. On my monthly visits home, I felt increasingly distant from my family and their way of life. My parents and siblings were living in a tent with no electricity, running water, or any of the other conveniences to which I had become accustomed at school. We saw things differently, and I felt that they didn't understand my needs. I asked questions that they couldn't answer. When I challenged or disagreed with them, they became angry and said that I had changed for the worse.

When I graduated from high school, my family expected me to become a teacher in the elementary school in our area, a job which was considered very high status at the time. It took some doing for me to persuade my father to let me attend university. He had no idea what university was. It wasn't until an uncle of mine, who worked on a kibbutz and knew what university was, interceded on my behalf that he gave his consent.

It was at university that my Westernization began in earnest. Whole worlds were opened up to me in my classes, as well as by the Jewish friends I made. I took part in their conversations, was invited to their parties, and was made welcome in their homes. My professors were also remarkably forthcoming. My university experience affected me in more ways than I can enumerate, but I think that the major one was that it turned me into a questioning individual with ideas and opinions of my own. I could no longer accept things without examining them, and I could no longer keep my peace just because my elders believed differently. I also lost any belief I might have had in amulets, sorcery, and the evil eye.

I completed my B.A. in social work before the days of "cultural sensitivity." The models of social work intervention that were taught, and the values, skills, and epistemologies underlying them, were entirely Western. It did not occur to me or, probably, to anyone else at the university that they might not be entirely suited to work with non-Western peoples. I assumed that I would go back to the Negev and simply apply my new and shining knowledge.

Yet, though I was proud of my Bedouin-Arab roots and deeply committed to helping my people, my professional training had created a gulf between us. In any professional relationship, there is bound to be a gap between patient and helper since it is impossible to completely transcend the inevitable differences in experience and social location that distinguish the two. But for me, the gap was exacerbated by the Western acculturation which removed me from my roots and from my people and their perception of illness.

Over an eleven-year period, from 1981 to 1992, 1 worked with the Bedouin-Arab population of the Negev in two settings:

1. In the Department of Psychiatry in the general hospital of Soroka Medical Centre in Beer-Sheva, the capital of the Negev.

2. In the main primary health care center in the Bedouin-Arab city of Rahat.

At the hospital, I was the first and only Arab mental health professional; at the clinic I was the only mental health professional.

With my Israeli training and Western approach, my thinking was like that of any Western therapist. I tended to analyze the patients' difficulties "scientifically" and to ignore their belief systems, cultural patterns, and perceptions of their illness or problems.

These behaviors were strongly reinforced by the Jewish, Arab, and Bedouin-Arab GPs with whom I worked. They, like myself, tended to ignore traditional Bedouin-Arab modes of healing. Most derided their patients' experiences with traditional healers. All treated and communicated with their patients through their symptoms. They showed little social awareness or gender sensitivity and paid little attention to what was behind the symptoms—behaviors which have been reported by others as well (Abdul-Menaim, 1991; Walker, 1995).

Some of their conduct was quite callous. For example, one Bedouin-Arab GP, in telling his colleagues about a Bedouin-Arab woman who was unable to indicate the location of her pain for which he found no medical reasons, actually mimicked her. Other physicians would mockingly tell of how their female patients complained about heartache while pointing to their stomachs. None of the staff appreciated the cultural reasons why a Bedouin-Arab woman would not point to her breasts. I didn't enlighten them. With my admiration for their learning and status, I wanted to be one of them, so I shared their disdain.

It is not surprising that the physicians I worked with were not particularly successful in dealing with their Bedouin-Arab patients' mental health problems. Many patients left feeling hurt, angry, and bewildered. One, I recall, was outraged that his GP demanded that he throw away the amulet he was wearing. More than a few were upset with the contempt the physicians showed for the power of the healers and, they believed, for God.

I wasn't very successful either. For the first few years of my work, my encounters with my patients were a bitter comedy of cross-expectations. In contrast to what I had been taught to expect, my patients did not come to me for help with their "emotional" problems. Without exception, they were all referred to me by a physician, usually a GP, though sometimes a psychiatrist, with physical symptoms for which there was no medical explanation. They called me "Doctor" and expected a physical examination and medication.

True to my training, I tried to uncover the roots of their somatization by asking them about their personal and family lives. Most of them were disinclined to tell me. Some of them became extremely upset when I told them that they had no physical problems and that their symptoms arose from psychosocial or psychiatric causes. "What, do you think I'm crazy?" was not an uncommon response. Other clients simply ignored the information. Many terminated treatment after one or two sessions. The few who persisted wanted to know what the connection was between their symptoms and the personal questions I asked them. My efforts at explanation—telling them that their problems stemmed from traumas or developments in their youth—only made them more upset.

Moreover, whatever their gender, education, or social class, at the end of my initial evaluation, they invariably asked, "Now what are you going to do?" Their emphasis was on the second person, the practitioner. As they saw it, they had told me their problem and it was my job to treat it. One woman, on learning that my treatment would be to talk with her, informed me bluntly that she had other people to talk with and didn't need me for this.

The literature refers, with some frustration, to the "resistance" of Arab mental health patients who apparently refuse to assume responsibility for their illnesses or problems (Mass & Al-Krenawi, 1994; Devore & Schlesinger, 1991; West, 1987). 1 felt similarly stymied by their attitude.

To make matters worse, I was so cut off from our shared culture that I ignored the obvious. I had forgotten how much Bedouin-Arabs speak in metaphors and ignored it when clients told me of their distress using popular proverbs. For example, when a young unmarried male client told me that he was "a baby camel left alone in the desert," I didn't pick up his feelings of abandonment. Nor did I ask what he meant. Similarly, I paid no attention to the strong interdiction against Bedouin-Arab women making eye contact with men, so when my female patients kept their eyes averted, I interpreted it as resistance. I also put out of my mind the fact that women in mourning wear blue embroidery on their dresses, so I didn't connect the depression of one of my patients with her bereavement.

These are only a few examples of the meanings I missed. Looking back on them, I attribute my obtuseness to a combination of training that did not include cross-cultural awareness, a matter which did not reach Israel until many years after it was commonplace in Social Work schools in the United States and England, and my own very hefty dose of denial of my connection to my Bedouin-Arab roots. On both counts, it was easier for me to search for the "facts" and "information" that I had been taught to look for.

I also ignored everything having to do with traditional views of illness. When my clients told me that they were possessed by demons or the evil eye—agents of mental illness in Bedouin-Arab culture—I ignored the revelations. Nor did 1 pay attention to my patients' terminology of mental illness, even though I actually knew what it meant. Thus, when a client told me that he was afflicted by "air from evil spirits" (in Arabic *Nafasmn Al-Jinn*), it took me some time to acknowledge that she was depressed. When I was told that another patient had been "attacked from evil spirits inhabiting the earth" (in Arabic, *Darbaat Blaad*), I didn't immediately translate the statement into the Western terminology that she was psychotic. I now know what traditional healers mean when they say that evil spirits from the earth have entered a person's body.

For several years, I was unhappy with my work and angry with the people I served. I also felt frustrated professionally. I wanted to make a career as a clinical social worker, and these people weren't letting me. I began to wonder whether Bedouin-Arabs had any use for social workers. I even began to entertain thoughts of working with Jewish clients, who, I believed, would better understand what I was doing and would be better for my career as well.

Feeling increasingly dissatisfied with the way I was helping, or not helping, my clients, I began to sense that things would have to change. But I didn't know what or how. I had been given no precedents, had no mentors, and the skills I had learned only partially equipped me for what lay ahead. For a long time, I felt caught between my hurt at the doctors' attitudes towards my people and my anger and frustration at my Bedouin-Arab patients for not behaving in the ways I expected.

It took me a long time to shift my focus to myself, though, and to wonder whether and how I could do things differently. Finally, after about five years of banging my head against the wall as most of my patients refused to engage in "talking therapy" and terminated after one or two sessions, it dawned on me that the responsibility might not be all theirs. In a burst of desperation and hard won humility, I decided to ask my father what he thought. Our relationship was much better now than it had been when I was an alienated adolescent and he was trying to cope with a rebellious son. Both my parents were very proud of me when I graduated from university and began to work at the clinic, and I now enjoyed listening to my father tell his stories about the Bedouin-Arabs and their way of life. At this point, his lack of schooling, and the fact that he had no more idea than my clients of what a social worker does, struck me as a positive advantage.

After listening to my predicament, he gave me two pieces of advice. One came embedded in a Bedouin-Arab proverb: "Don't walk against the wind. If you do, you're going to lose. You have to walk cautiously with the wind to find a way out." This proverb, which draws for its emotional force on the foolhardiness of walking headlong into a desert sandstorm, conveyed the message that change can be made by going with nature, or reality, not against it. That is, change must be made slowly, carefully, and with awareness of and respect for the circumstances.

The other piece of advice was: "You're riding an airplane; the people you're talking about are walking on foot." Telling me not to regard my patients from the lordly position of my superior education but from their own position, this point supplemented the first.

Though I understood the words, it took me a while to fully grasp what my father meant, and even longer to apply it. For about half a year, I struggled internally, looking for a way of translating his rich metaphors into the language of the profession I had learned. By the end of this period, my father's sayings brought me back in touch with some of the basic tenets of social work, which seem to have gone by the wayside in the years of frustrating practice:

1. Work with, not against, the clients and understand them in their own environment,
2. Avoid applying intervention techniques that are unfamiliar to the client.
3. Look for the clients' strengths and natural sources of help.
4. Think in terms of all the systems in which the clients are involved.
5. Accept the clients as they are and respect their belief systems.

In terms of my own work, it became clear to me that the distinction that my colleagues and I had made between "us" and "them," our Bedouin-Arab clients, was a false one. I realized that for all my efforts, most of my clients would never fully understand the knowledge and skills that I brought to my work, and that it was my job to bridge the gap. I finally realized that my professional task would have to be to integrate what I had learned into the cultural context of my people.

The next step was to figure out how to act on my new understandings. I began with the most basic of social work practices: asking and listening to my clients. In particular, I tried to elicit their perceptions of their illness and ways of dealing with it. Instead of looking for the etiology of their symptoms in their personal and family background as the first order of business, I would ask the patients themselves what they believed caused their problem. If their answer was demons or evil spirits, I now took their explanation seriously and inquired further. Why did the demons attack? How? What did they do and say? This would usually lead fairly quickly to the interpersonal and intrapsychic issues behind the symptoms.

I also began to pay more attention to traditional healing. Like the GPs I worked with, I knew that my clients consulted traditional healers before, during and after their modern treatment; but also like them, I ignored the "unscientific" practice. With my decision to leave the "airplane" and "walk with the wind," I began to accept the fact that the traditional healers were part of my patients' lives, and I set out to learn more about them.

At first, my patients refused to tell me anything. They were afraid of revealing secret knowledge involving their communication with supernatural powers and jeopardizing their treatment or being punished for it. Also, they didn't trust me very much. As one healer said rather bluntly: "You belong to the university and clinic. No one on your side believes in what we do. You laugh at our treatment. All the people I see had been at the hospital first, and none of them felt that their symptoms improved till they came to see us." Luckily, my uncle happens to be sheik of our tribe, and he was willing to vouch for me. This opened the door to the male healers who, after some negotiations, agreed to share their knowledge and experience with me, excluding some sensitive areas of their practice, such as the language of the evil spirits and the healers' communication with supernatural powers.

The doors of the female healers were still closed to me, though. To open them, I asked their husbands for permission to meet with their healer wives but was turned down. Then I brought my mother along. She promised their husbands that she would accompany me to all the meetings and act as a kind of chaperone. This got me entrance.

I encountered similar difficulties in getting my clients to talk about the healers they saw. One client I asked responded bluntly: "You don't respect this type of healing and laugh at it." Still, I persisted. When patients told me they had been attacked by evil spirits, I asked whether they had consulted a traditional healer. If they said that they had, I asked how the traditional healer diagnosed and treated their complaints. The approach worked wonders. Clients who would have clammed up had I asked them about their personal feelings and relationships suddenly opened up and shared things with me.

To give only one of many possible examples, I had a female client who started to suffer from various unexplained aches and pains after her husband took a second wife. In the past, I would have asked her to tell me what was bothering her or about her family life, and she would either have focused on her symptoms or left the treatment. But now I asked her how she explained her symptoms and whether she had done anything about them before her GP referred her to me. These questions unlocked her story. She told me that she had seen a traditional healer who had told her that her husband's new wife had done sorcery against her in order to create problems between her husband and herself. I didn't cast doubt on his evaluation, as I would have done in the past, and encouraged her to continue talking about the sorcery. My reward was that in talking about the sorcery, she revealed her anger at her husband and his second wife. She returned session after session, eager to vent her difficulties in her polygamous marriage.

Simultaneously, I approached traditional healers to learn how they viewed and treated mental illness and how they related to their patients. I even observed and participated in healing rituals that traditional healers performed on members of my extended family. For example, I joined my family in the common ritual of visiting a saint's tomb. I listened to the Koran reading and watched as candles and incense were lit beside the grave and a white cloth was hung on the tomb. I heard the vows made to appease the saints and to special requests to keep tragedy or illness from striking the supplicant and his family. I became aware of the potential in this and other healing rituals for self-expression, catharsis, ventilation, self-satisfaction, and psychological release.

Throughout it all, the driving question in my mind, though I never articulated it, was how could I, a Western-trained and, in many respects, a Western-thinking practitioner, use my knowledge and skills to understand the traditional healer's approach and integrate it into my own work?

Fortunately, I had two very good mentors in the professional community. One was Y. Bilu, whom I "met" through his 1978 study of ethnopsychiatry with Moroccan-born patients in Israel who used traditional healers. His findings, showing that traditional healing had a 70 percent success rate in this population, were both revealing and encouraging. This success rate is comparable to that of conventional Western psychiatry, and Bilu's discovery that traditional healers were as effective as Western ones bolstered my growing conviction that the traditional healers in my own community had a good deal to teach me. I was heartened, too, by Bilu's call for the integration of traditional healing into Western psychiatry. Bilu's pioneering work provided recognized, academic support for my own quest. It reinforced my sense that I was going in the right direction and wasn't working in a vacuum in my small, out-of-the way station in the Negev.

My other mentor was my supervisor at the Soroka hospital psychiatric clinic, the Jewish psychiatrist Dr. Maoz. Maoz was a humane and broad-minded physician who emphasized the need for "natural" empathy, patience, and devotion in treating emotional and interpersonal problems. He provided a personal example of a professional who spent time with his patients and their families, who was interested in more than their symptoms, and who made it a cardinal rule to form good relationships with the people he treated (Maoz et. al., 1992). While the GPs I worked with regarded my forays into traditional healing with amused skepticism, Maoz was all for them.

Both Bilu and Maoz strongly influenced my emerging sense of how one had to work with a Bedouin-Arab population. Each in his own way served as an example for me to follow. They also helped me throw off the erroneous assumption imparted in my professional training that the methods of social work practice are universally applicable. This method is a Western model that was adopted in most developing countries, but, as Al-Dabbagh (1993) points out, it has failed in Arab (Islamic) countries, due largely to its exclusion of religious values and spiritual considerations (Ragab, 1990). My own professional experience supports this claim.

When in 1988 I enrolled in an M.A. program in Social Work, I soon began to do formal research on the Bedouin-Arab approach to mental health. My Master's thesis, "The role of the Dervish as a mental health therapist in the Negev-Bedouin-Arab society: Clients' expectations from these treatments and the extent of materialization" (1992), was the first study that dealt with the subject in any depth. My choice of subject derived from my growing conviction that, as a social worker, I needed to understand the culture of my clients and especially its way of dealing with mental illness.

My research led me to spend yet more time visiting traditional healers. I sat with the patients while they waited for treatment, sometimes joined in their talk, and observed the incipient group dynamic that developed, through which they found relief by sharing their stories and problems. I participated in rituals in the healers' homes and watched the healers apply their therapy. I could do this because ritual healing, at least as the Bedouin-Arab know it, is carried out in public—unless the patient asks for privacy—in front of both the patient's own family and the patients and their families who are waiting their turn.

I saw something very different from anything that I was familiar with in a western clinic. For example, the Dervishes rarely asked questions of the patients. Instead, after ascertaining the cause of their illness by looking at their symptoms, touching their heads, or examining some item belonging to the patient, they would proceed to energetically expel the evil spirits. They would communicate, sometimes loudly and angrily, with the spirits and give the patient instructions. Sometimes they would even beat the spirits out of the patients. Throughout it all, the patients remained passive as the Dervish worked on them.

I also saw that the healers took care to assure the patients that their illness wasn't of their own making but something that came upon them from outside, whether directly from God or evil spirits or through the agency of sorcery or the evil eye. Being able to project their problem left the patients feeling good about themselves and strengthened their determination to fight the illness. I also realized that the healers and their patients share the same "poetic" terminology of illness that I had scorned.

As I learned, I gradually changed my entire approach. One major difference was that I became more active. Instead of asking my clients to talk about their lives, I gave instructions and advice. For example, when a mother came complaining of her son's enuresis, instead of trying to ascertain its cause, I simply instructed her on what to do to try to stop it. My approach became more cognitive, more behavioral, and more directive. I provided information about the illness or symptoms the patient presented and dealt directly to alleviate the symptoms. These methods of interventions met the patients' expectations and increased their trust of the practitioners' abilities to address their problems.

I incorporated some traditional practices into my work, which had the double advantage of being meaningful to my patients and of enabling me to play an active role. For example, in a group I led, I helped Bedouin-Arab widows to deal with their survivor guilt manifested in fears that they would be killed by the spirits of their dead husbands, by having them carry out the traditional mourning ritual (in Arabic *Rahama*) and then discussing their experiences and the feelings that the ritual had raised or resolved (Al-Krenawi and Graham, 1996). Most of the widows I did this with felt relieved afterwards and no longer had nightmares of their dead husbands coming to attack them. With other patients, I visited saints' tombs, after having done this with my own fancily as I described above. Saints' tombs are holy places, and visiting them is traditionally used to relieve personal anxiety, heal physical and mental ailments, and mediate requests to God (Al-Krenawi & Graham, 1996; El-Islam, 1967). Although I myself do not believe in spirits or sorcery, I could feel in myself and recognize in my patients the sense of belonging, safety, and relief that these rituals afforded.

Another traditional practice I turned to was to elicit the assistance of family members in my work with patients (Al-Krenawi, 1995a, 1995b; Al-Krenawi & Graham, 1996; Al-Krenawi et. al., 1995; Graham & Al-Krenawi, 1996; Mass & Al-Krenawi, 1994). The mourning ritual involved, among other things, a ceremonial family meal. A more specific instance was in the case of a patient suffering from hallucinations brought on by an argument with his mother in which he nearly hit her, an act which so violates Bedouin-Arab behavioral norms that it is considered sinful. In this case, I arranged for a reconciliation between the patient and his mother in the presence of his brothers. The reconciliation followed my use of accepted Western techniques: paradoxical techniques to alleviate the patient's terrors of the malevolent spirits of his hallucinations, and role playing to clarify his feelings of guilt and expectations of punishment for his act (Al-Krenawi & Graham, 1997).

I also let my clients know that I accepted their concurrent utilization of traditional healers. I asked how their traditional healers viewed their problems and tried to make use of their perceptions. Sometimes I accompanied patients to their healers or consulted the healer directly about the patient. In the case of the patient discussed above, following the reconciliation with his mother, I urged the family to arrange a visit to a Dervish to expel the evil spirits because the patient viewed the spirits to which he attributed his illness as having been sent by Allah to punish him for his disrespect. This meant that, to the patient, only someone with supernatural powers could free him of the spirits. I should note that it was not necessary for me to believe in spirits, in the healer's supernatural powers, or in the "exorcism" he performed, but only to accept that the patient did and to treat his belief with respect.

A related change was that I became more careful about intimating that a patient's disorder had an internal cause, an etiology which implies that the disorder is somehow of his or her own doing and evokes a great deal of anger, shame, and denial. Thus, as evident in the above example, I ceased to challenge the common Bedouin-Arab view that mental disturbance is caused by supernatural powers (rather than internal conflicts). I did not engage in "insight" therapy or try to confront patients directly with their rage, guilt, and other culturally unacceptable emotions, but rather allowed them to resolve these feelings actively. For example, the reconciliation I facilitated between the patient discussed above and his mother enabled expiation, while the use of the Dervish provided a culturally acceptable way of closing the chapter on his anger.

I also began to relate differently to my patients. With male patients, I removed some of the patient-therapist barriers. I chatted with them in the waiting room. I moved the table in my office which had separated us and let them sit closer to me. With my female patients, I stopped trying to make eye contact. I also adopted the traditional healers' quasi-familial terms of address. I called my unmarried female patients "sister," my middle aged matron patients "auntie," and my elderly women patients "grandma"—terms which encouraged the patients to see me as a concerned, protective family figure who would take care of them. This too made them more ready to open up.

I learned to communicate with my patients. I came to understand and build on their indirect ways of talking about themselves. When they talked in proverbs, I would try to interpret the proverb or ask them what it meant, and this would lead to a discussion of the feelings and experiences behind the proverb. I learned their terminology of illness, and although I didn't use it myself, I found that knowing the names and explanations that traditional healers give to patients' disorders helped me relay to the patients the modern diagnoses. Interestingly, traditional healers also distinguish between neurosis and psychosis, or minor and major mental health disorders. In the healers' classification, patients attacked by evil spirits which did not enter their body suffer from what they call an "easy" (in Arabic *khafif*) disorder. Those who behave bizarrely are believed to have been attacked by evil spirits which did enter their body, and are diagnosed as having a "difficult" (in Arabic *saab*) disorder (Al-Krenawi et al., 1995; Hes, 1975). In any case, in my discussions with patients of how they saw their illness—its causes and development—I could learn about their feelings and aspects of their intimate lives. It was no longer necessary for me to ask them directly about their family lives and personal relationships.

My new understanding also helped me to cope with the "resist-ance" that had previously so thwarted my efforts at helping. I came to realize that what the literature labeled "resistance" was not resistance in the psychoanalytic understanding of the term, but rather a reflection of the bewilderment that my Bedouin-Arab patients felt at the non-directives of the Western practitioner and of their culture-bound expec-tation that the practitioner take an active role in the healing (Al-Krenawi, 1992). Once I became aware of this, I could deal with their attitude as a culturally based expectation. I could let my clients know that I under-stood where their lack of being forthcoming stemmed from and could work to create the trust that they needed to let me into their personal lives. The fact that many fewer clients now terminated their treatment after one or two sessions told me I was on the right track.

● Can Traditional and Modern Mental Health Care be Integrated?

My thesis findings—that many patients utilized traditional healing alongside modern medical care and that the majority of the Dervishes' patients were satisfied with their traditional treatment (Al-Krenawi, 1992)—caused me to wonder. What, I asked myself, was wrong with the "modern" mode of helping? What was right about the "traditional" practices? Could the two co-exist in harmony? Could they perhaps nur-ture and support one another?

In my own practice, I've found that they can. Research in the field bolsters this conclusion. The anthropological study of traditional healing has gone through two broad phases. The first focused on the question of whether healers or shamans were themselves mentally ill, namely schizophrenic or epileptic. By the 1950s and 1960s, it was concluded that they were not. The shift in assessment is actually similar to the one that I had undergone. In the second phase, anthropologists began to look into the similarities between shamans and psychotherapists. The explicitly religious dimensions of the traditional healing practices were pushed into the background (Fernando, 1991) and shamans have come to be increasingly perceived in Western countries as healer-psychotherapists (Jilek, 1971). Their techniques, such as suggestion and persuasion, are described as similar to those used by psychiatrists (Frank, 1973; Kiev, 1964; Nelson & Torrey, 1973; Ruiz & Langrod, 1976a). Some researchers (Bravo & Grob, 1989) even urge psychiatrists to be more open to learn from shamans.

A fair number of studies point to psychotherapeutic elements in traditional healing (Al-Krenawi & Graham, 1996; Atkinson, 1987; Bankart et. al., 1992; Daie et. al., 1992), among them catharsis, ventilation, and relaxation (Levi-Strauss, 1963; Scheff, 1979). Traditional healing rituals, it has been suggested, work by establishing a homology between the symbolic and the experiential in which the former metaphorically transforms the latter by triggering a non-specific mechanism such as suggestion, catharsis, or placebo effect; by offering social support or the resolution of social conflict; and/or by transforming the meaning of affliction for the sufferer through a ritually powerful, symbolic performance (Scheff, 1979).

Moreover, studies show that, much like modern mental health care, traditional healing tackles problems at the various levels of the individual, family, group, and community (El-Islam, 1967; Grotberg, 1990; Hajal, 1987; Kennedy, 1967; Napoliello & Sweet, 1992). As modern services became available, these overlaps have enabled clients of various ethnic affiliations to integrate the traditional services with the new ones, though they often do so without telling their Western clinicians (Nyamwaya, 1987; Rankin & Kappy, 1993; Waldman, 1990).

For the most part, this patient-initiated model of integration between traditional and modern health care is one-directional. While traditional healers are quite interested in learning about what goes on in modern health care, Western-trained mental health practitioners tend not to be interested in traditional healing (Al-Krenawi, 1995b). Rarely has the interactive process in traditional healing been considered in detail; even more rarely has the experiential process been examined; and almost never has a systematic comparison between traditional healing and psychotherapy been attempted.

Moreover, although family and community rituals are sometimes used in counseling and psychotherapy, they have rarely been identified as part of the psychotherapeutic process (cf. Palazzoli et. al., 1978; Van der Hart et. al., 1988). Generally they are relegated to the status of a task that the therapist assigns the client, with no acknowledgment or explanation of their therapeutic purpose (Yalom, 1975). Even in the rare cases where rituals have been given legitimacy in therapy (Renner, 1979), there are few detailed accounts of how, when, and why they are used. A notable exception is Rando's (1985) article outlining his clinical observations.

My personal experience supports the positions that mental health practitioners would do well (1) to learn about, value, and show respect for their clients' cultures, and especially for their traditional and religious approaches to psychological healing; and (2) in their own practice to draw upon and support the conjoint use of the traditional healing methods (e.g., rituals) in the patient's religion and culture (Azhar et. al., 1994). My main point is that, in view of the commonalities in the modern and traditional healing approaches, both mental health workers and, more importantly, their patients would probably benefit from their integration. Indeed, many researchers have called for integrating modern and traditional healing (Ezeji & Sarvela, 1992; Heilman & Witztum, 1994; LaFromboise et. al., 1990; Jilek, 1994; Lambo, 1978; Lin et. al., 1990; Ogunremi, 1987; Schwartz, 1985; Wessels, 1985). My experience supports this call.

● Guidelines for Bridging the Gap

Although modern and traditional models of helping conflict with one another at many points, the task of social workers who treat traditional clients is to approach with an open mind both them and the traditional healing the clients utilize. Only thus can we hope to win the trust that is essential to truly helping them. Instead of rejecting the traditional healers for their reliance on supernatural powers, we should give thought to what traditional modes of helping we can incorporate into our work and how we can do so.

The following guidelines are suggested as means to obtaining the information that is necessary if we are to treat our traditional clients in their own contexts and to make use of the healing resources of their culture:

1. We should seek to understand the client's culture, religion, values, and belief system.
2. In taking the client's history, we should try to learn more about his or her nuclear and extended family, asking questions such as: What are the relationships among the family members? Under what circumstances do they meet? Who are the authority figures? What are the family rituals?
3. We should investigate the relationship with the community, asking questions such as: Who is the respected spiritual leader (i.e. the rabbi, priest, sheik, or traditional healer)? Are there any community rituals, and what is their purpose?
4. We should investigate self-treatment: Does the client understand the symptoms? How does he or she deal with them? What sources has he or she consulted, i.e., family or community members, religious-spiritual leaders, traditional healers?
5. In addressing symptomatology, we should consider the client's own interpretation as well as how persons in the client's family and community assess the symptoms—that is, their tentative diagnosis and etiological explanation.
6. We should find out what treatment the traditional healers suggested and what their diagnosis means from the client's perspective.
7. We should investigate the social construction (and legitimacy) of the sick role in the client's family and community (including the patient's rights and obligations).

The above information can help us to select the appropriate intervention techniques. For example, if we know who the authorities in the client's nuclear and extended family and community are, we can enlist them in our intervention (Al-Krenawi et al., 1994; Heilman & Witztum, 1994; Lum, 1982).

8. Lastly, in keeping with the client's expectations, we should adopt an active and directive role in the treatment sessions.

In sum, traditional healing may be highly useful for mental health practitioners who work with non-Western ethnic groups. Western and traditional healing are complementary and should be constructed to function alongside one another (Chi, 1994; Green & Makhulu, 1979; Rappaport & Rappaport, 1981). Because social work intervention is often based on intuitive as well as empirical knowledge, traditional healing can readily be integrated into practice with people of various cultures (Applewhite, 1995; Castellano, Et. Al., 1986; Gutheil, 1993; Kissman, 1990; Laird, 1984; Morrissette, et. al., 1993; Schindler, 1993). An understanding of the many and deep connections between modern and traditional healing approaches should enable Western practitioners to collaborate with their non-Western clients in the therapeutic process and, with them, search for viable resolutions of their difficulties in a culturally respectful manner.

● References

Abdul-Menaim, F. (1991). Medical practice in rural Egypt: Anthropological study in an Egyptian village. In S. Ottman. N. Abdul-Hameed. F. Abdul-Rahman (Eds.), *Health and illness.* (pp. 117–172). Alexandria: Daar Al-Marif Al-Jamiah (in Arabic).

Abu-Khusa, A. (1994). *The tribes of Beer-Sheva.* Amman: Al-Matbah Al-Wataniah (in Arabic).

Al-Dabbagh, A. (1993). Islamic perspectives on social work practice. *The American Journal of Islamic Social Sciences, 10*(4), 536–537.

Al-Haj, M. (1989). Social research on family lifestyles among Arabs in Israel. *Journal of Comparative Studies, 20*(2), 175–195.

Al-Issa, I. (1990). Culture and mental illness in Algeria. *International Journal of Social Psychiatry, 36*(3), 230–240.

Al-Krenawi, A. (1992). *The role of the Dervish as a mental health therapist in the Negev-Bedouin-Arab society: Client's expectations from these treatments and the extent of materialization.* Unpublished MSW thesis, Hebrew University of Jerusalem (in Hebrew).

Al-Krenawi, A. (1995a). *A study of dual use of modern and traditional mental health systems by the Bedouin-Arab of the Negev.* Unpublished Ph.D. dissertation, University of Toronto.

Al-Krenawi, A. (1995b). *The making of a healer: From mental patient to therapist in Israeli Bedouin-Arab Society.* Paper presented at the Qualitative Research Conference, Studying Social Life: Ethnography in Cross-Cultural Perspective: Hamilton, Ontario, Canada (May 30–June 2).

Al-Krenawi, A., & Graham, J. (1996). Social work and traditional healing rituals among the Bedouin of the Negev, Israel. *International Social Work, 39*(2), 177–188.

Al-Krenawi, A., & Graham, J. (1997). Spirit possession and exorcism in the treatment of a Bedouin psychiatric patient. *Clinical Social Work Journal, 25*(2), 211–222.

Al-Krenawi, A., Maoz, B., & Shiber, A. (1995). Integration of modern medical methods with popular methods in treating mental-disorders in Bedouin-Arab. *Sihot-Dialogue, Israel Journal of Psychotherapy, 10*(1), 42–48 (in Hebrew).

Al-Krenawi, A., Maoz, B., & Riecher, B. (1994). Familial and cultural issues in the brief strategic treatment of Israeli Bedouin. *Family Systems Medicine, 12*(4), 415–425.

Al-Sadawi, N. (1977). *Arab women and their psychological struggle.* Beirut: Al-Moassah Al-Arabiah (in Arabic).

Applewhite, S. L. (1995). Curenderismo: Demystifying health beliefs and practices of elderly Mexican Americans. *Health & Social Work, 20*(4), 247–253.

Atkinson, J. M. (1987). The effectiveness of shamans in an Indonesian ritual. *American Anthropologist, 89*(2), 342–355.

Azhar, M. Z., Varma, S. L., & Dharap, A. S. (1994). Religious psychotherapy in anxiety disorder patients. *Acta Psychiatrica Scandinavica, 90*(1), 1–3.

Bankart, C., Koshikawa, F., Nedate, K., & Haruki, Y. (1992). When West meets East: Contributions of Eastern traditions to the future of psychotherapy. *Psychotherapy, 29*(1), 141–149.

Ben-Asa, B. (1974). The Bedouin patient. *Journal of the Israel Medical Association, 78*(2), 73–76 (in Hebrew).

Bilu, Y. (1978). *Traditional psychiatry in Israel: Moroccan born Moshav members with psychiatric disorders and "problems in living", and their traditional healers.* Unpublished Ph.D. thesis, Hebrew University of Jerusalem (in Hebrew).

Bokan, J. A., & Campbell, W. (1984). Indigenous psychotherapy in the treatment of a Laotian refugee. *Hospital and Community Psychiatry, 35*(3), 281–282.

Bravo, G., & Grob, C. (1989). Shamans, sacraments, and psychiatrists. *Journal of Psychoactive Drugs, 21*(1), 123–128.

Burgest, R. D. (1982). Overviews: Implication for social theory and Third World people. In R. D. Burgest (Ed.), *Social work with minorities.* (pp.45–56). London: The Scarecrow Press, Inc.

Castellano, M. B., Stalwick, H., & Wien, F. (1986). Native social work education in Canada: Issues and adaptations. *Canadian Social Work Review, 4,*166–184.

Chaleby, K. (1987). Women of polygamous marriages in outpatient psychiatric services in Kuwait. *International Journal of Family Psychiatry, 8*(1), 25–34.

Chamie, J. (1986). Polygyny among Arabs. Population Studies, 40(1), 55–66.

Chi, C. (1994). Integrating traditional medicine into modern health care systems: Examining the role of Chinese medicine in Taiwan. *Social Science and Medicine, 39*(3), 307–321.

Daie, N., Witztum, E., Mark, M., & Rabinowitz, S. (1992). The belief in the transmigration of souls: Psychotherapy of a Druze patient with sever anxiety reaction. *British Journal of Medical Psychology, 65*(2), 119–130.

Devore, W., & Schlesinger, E. (1991). *Ethnic-sensitive social work practice* (3d Edition). New York: Macmillan.

Edwards, S. D. (1986). Traditional and modern medicine in South Africa: A research study. *Social Science and Medicine, 22*(11), 1273–1276.

El-Islam, M. F. (1967). The psychotherapeutic basis of some Arab rituals. *International Journal of Social Psychiatry, 13,* 265–68.

Erikson, E. (1963). *Childhood and society.* New York: Norton.

Ezeji, P. N., & Sarvela, P. D. (1992). Health care behaviour of the Ibo tribes of Nigeria. *Health Values the Journal of Health Behaviour, Education and Promotion, 16*(6), 31–35.

Fernando, S. (1991). *Mental health, race and culture.* London: Macmillan in association with Mind.

Frank, J. D. (1973). *Persuasion and healing: A comparative study of psychotherapy.* Baltimore: Johns Hopkins University Press.

Fromm, E. (1976). *To have or to be.* New York: Harper and Row.

Graham, J., & Al-Krenawi, A. (1996). A comparison study of traditional helpers in a late nineteenth century Canadian (Christian) society and late twentieth century Bedouin (Muslim) society in the Negev, Israel. *Journal of Multicultural Social Work, 4*(2), 31–48.

Green, E. C., & Makhulu. C. (1979). Traditional healers in Swaziland: Toward improved co-operation between the traditional and modern health sectors. *Social Science and Medicine, 18,* 1071–1079.

Green, J. W. (1982). Cultural awareness in the human services. Englewood Cliffs, N.J.: Prentice-Hall.

Grotberg, E. H. (1990). Mental health aspects of the Zar for women in Sudan. *Women and Therapy, 10*(3), 15–24.

Gutheil, I. A. (1993). Rituals and termination procedures. *Smith-College-Studies-in-Social Work, 63*(2), 163–176.

Hajal, F. (1987). Antecedent of family therapy: The family approach in traditional healing. *American Journal of Social Psychiatry, 7*(1), 42–46.

Hall, E. (1976). *Beyond culture.* New York: Doubleday.

Hebrew Encyclopedia, Vol. 7. (1954). Tel-Aviv: Reshafim Press (in Hebrew).

Heilman, S., & Witztum, E. (1994). Patients, chaperons and healers: Enlarging the therapeutic encounter. *Social Science and Medicine, 39*(1), 133–143.

Hes, P. J. (1975). Shamanism and psychotherapy. *Psychotherapy, 25,* 251–253.

Hofstede, G. (1989). Cultural differences in teaching and learning. *International journal of Intercultural Relations, 10*(3), 301–320.

Jilek, W. G. (1994). Traditional healing in the prevention and treatment of alcohol and drug abuse. *Transcultural Psychiatric Research Review, XXXI*(31), 219–256.

Jilek, W. G. (1971). From crazy witch doctor to auxiliary psychotherapist: The changing image of medicine man. *Psychiatric Clinic, 4,* 200–220.

Kennedy, J. G. (1967). Nubian Zar ceremonies as psychotherapy. *Human Organization, 26*(4), 185–194.

Kiev, A. (Ed.). (1964). *Magic, faith and healing, studies in primitive psychiatry today.* (pp.3–35). New York: Free Press.

Kissman, K. (1990). The role of fortune telling as a supportive function among Icelandic women. *International Social Work, 33*(2), 137–144.

Koltko, M. E. (1990). Religious beliefs affect psychotherapy the example of Mormonism. *Psychotherapy, 27,* 132–139.

Koss-Chioino, J. (1992). *Women as healers, women as patients: Mental health care and traditional healing in Puerto Rico.* San Francisco: Westview press.

LaFromboise, T. D., Trimble, J. E., & Mohatt, G. V. (1990). Counseling intervention and American Indian traditional: An integrative approach. *Counseling Psychologist, 18*(4), 628–654.

Laird, J. (1984). Sorcerers, shamans, and social workers: The use of ritual in social work practice. *Social Work, 29*(2), 123–129.

Lambo, T. A. (1978). Psychotherapy in Africa. *Human Nature, 1,* 32–40.

Lefley, H. P. (1986). Why cross-cultural training? Applied issues in culture and mental health service delivery. In H. P. Lefely & P. B. Pedersen (Eds.), *Cross-cultural training for mental health professionals.* (pp.11–44). Springfield, IL: Charles Thomas Publisher.

Levi-Strauss, C. (1963). The effectiveness of symbols. In C. Levi-Strauss, *Structural anthropology* (pp.181–201). New York: Anchor Books.

Lin, K. M., Demonteverde, L., & Nuccio, 1. (1990). Religion, healing, and mental health among Filipino Americans. *International Journal of Mental Health, 19*(3), 40–44.

Lum, D. (1982). Toward a framework for social work practice with minorities. *Social Work, 27*(3), 244–249.

Mahler, M. (1968). *On human symbiosis and the vicissitude of individuation: Infantile psychosis (vol. 1).* New York: International University Press.

Maoz, B., Rabinowitz, S., Merz, M., & Katz, H. E. (1992). *Doctors and their feelings: A pharmacological of medical caring.* Westport, Connecticut: Preager.

Mass, M., & Al-Krenawi, A. (1994). When a man encounters a woman, Satan is also present: Clinical relationships in Bedouin society. *American Journal of Orthopsychiatry, 64*(3), 357–367.

Morrissette, B., Morrissette, B., McKenzie, B., & Morrissette, L. (1993). Towards an aboriginal model of social work practice: Cultural knowledge and traditional practice. *Canadian Social Work Review, 10*(1), 91–107.

Napoliello, A. L., & Sweet, E. S. (1992). Salvador Minuchin's structural family therapy and its application to Native Americans. *Family Therapy, 19*(2), 255–165.

Nelson, S. H., & Torrey, F. E. (1973). The religious functions of psychiatry. *American Journal of Orthopsychiatry, 43*(3), 362–367.

New, P. K. (1977). Traditional and modern health care: An appraisal of complementarity. *International Social Science journal, XXIX*(3), 483–495.

Nyamwaya, D. (1987). A case study of the interaction between indigenous and western medicine among the Pokot of Kenya. *Social Science and Medicine, 25*(12), 1277–1287.

Ogunremi, 0. (1987). Community mental health in Nigeria: Challenge to the counselor and the behavioral scientist. *Nigerian Journal of Guidance and Counseling, 3*(1–2), 43–49.

Palazzoli, M. S., Boscolo, U. L., Cecchin, G., & Prata, G. (1978). *Paradox and counterparadox: A new model in the therapy of the family in schizophrenic transaction.* New York: Jason Aronson.

Pedersen, P. B., Fukuyama, M., & Heath, A. (1989). Client, counselor, and contextual variables in multicultural counseling. In B. Pedersen, J. G. Draguns, W. J. Lonner, & J. E. Trimle (Eds.), *Counseling across cultures* (3rd ed.). Honolulu: University of Hawaii Press.

Ragab, I. (1990). How can social work really take roots in developing countries. *Social Development Issues, 12*(3), 221–230.

Rando, T. A. (1985). Creating therapeutic rituals in the psychotherapy of the bereaved. *Psychotherapy, 22*(2), 236–240.

Rankin, S. B., & Kappy, M. S. (1993). Developing therapeutic relationships in multicultural settings. *Academic Medicine, 68*(11), 826–827.

Rappaport, H., & Rappaport, M. (1981). The integration of scientific and traditional healing: A proposed model. *American Psychologist, 36*(7), 774–781.

Renner, H. P. (1979). The use of ritual in a pastoral care. *The Journal of Pastoral Care, 33,* 166–174.

Ruiz, P., & Langrod, J. (1976a). The role of folk healers in community mental health services. *Community Mental Health, 12*(4), 392–398.

Ruiz, P., & Langrod, J. (1976b). Psychiatry and folk healing: A dichotomy? *American Journal of Psychiatry, 133*(1), 95–97.

Scheff, T. (1979). *Catharsis in healing, ritual and drama.* Berekely: University of California Press.

Schindler, R. (1993). Emigration and the black Jews of Ethiopia: Dealing with bereavement and loss. *International Social Work, 36*(1), 7–19.

Schwartz, D. (1985). Caribbean folk beliefs and Western psychiatry. *Journal of Psychosocial Nursing and Mental Health Services, 23*(11), 26–30.

Sue, D. W., & Sue, D. (1990). *Counseling the culturally different: Theory and practice.* (2d ed.). New York: John Wiley and Sons.

Van der Hart, O., Witztum, E., & de-Voogt, A. (1988). Myth and rituals: Anthropological views and their application in strategic family therapy. *Journal of Psychotherapy and the Family, 4*(3/4), 57–79.

Waldman, J. B. (1990). Access to traditional medicine in a western Canadian city. *Medical Anthropology, 12*(3), 325–348.

Walker, L. (1995). The practice of primary health care: A case study. *Social Science and Medicine, 40*(6), 815–824.

Wessels, W. H. (1985). The traditional healer and psychiatry. *Australian and New Zealand Journal of Psychiatry, 19*(3), 283–286.

West, J. (1987). Psychotherapy in the Eastern province of Saudi Arabia. *Psychotherapy, 24*(1), 105–107.

Yalom, I. D. (1975). *The theory and practice of group psychotherapy* (2d ed.). New York: Basic Books.

Yoder, P. S. (1982). Biomedical and ethnomedical practice in rural Zaire. *Social Science and Medicine, 16,* 1851–1858.

● Reflective Inquiry

1. Would you consider using any of the non-traditional approaches presented by the author in your practice? Explain.

2. What are your thoughts and judgments of the author's "guidelines" for using the healing resources he suggests can truly help persons?

3. Under what, if any conditions, would you consider using "traditional" healers, such as described by the author? Explain.

Honoring Angels in My Path: Spiritually Sensitive Group Work with Persons Who Are Incarcerated

by Michael J. Sheridan, Ph.D.

This narrative tells the story of working with a group of men who are incarcerated on issues related to the process of recovery. Glimpses of the group's evolving sense of purpose and connection are provided to illustrate how spirituality can be interwoven with the process of professional helping.

● The Process of Noticing

A movie about angels started the process. Actually, the seeds had been planted long before, but it was the movie's message that stirred the seeds toward expression. My husband and I were driving home after

Most of the men's real first names have been used in this narrative as specifically requested by them. As one man stated, expressing the sentiment of the group, "I've had my name connected with negative things in the past. I want my name associated with something positive now." I have honored their request. One man who was involved early in the life of the group cannot be contacted; thus, a pseudonym is used.

I gratefully acknowledge the participation of the men of the RESPECT Recovery Group at Nottoway Correctional Center—Abbey, Andre, Frankie, Keith, Lennie, Marvin, Paul, Rashid, Red, Saleem, Spellman, Sylvester, Wallace, William, and Vernon—for both the many gifts they've brought to our group and for their valuable review of this manuscript. Also greatly appreciated is the support and talent of the group's two co-facilitators, Mr. Michael Crosby and Mr. Charles Clay, as well as their helpful review of this narrative.

seeing the movie "Heart and Souls." As is our custom, we talked about the movie's overall theme and its lesson. The plot was simple. At the exact moment that a baby boy is born in a car, four adults lose their lives as the trolley car they are riding in careens off a bridge to the street below. The souls of these persons intersect with the baby's new spirit at the moment of birth, and from that moment on they become his special angels. Only he can see and hear them, and the five "hearts and souls" become bonded for some purpose that none of them understand. Later on in the movie, they discover that the boy, now a man, is meant to help the four souls complete the unfinished business they left behind as a result of their untimely deaths. Once the task is accomplished, each soul is released to continue on his or her journey, and the man left behind learns a great deal about his own true spirit in the process. My husband and I decided that the theme of the movie was about noticing when significant people "cross your path" and honoring that intersection.

The movie tugged at a part of me that had been lying dormant for some time. As a junior faculty member working toward tenure, I had been focusing on my academic life at the expense of several other facets of my life. I feared that my only major contribution had been to move hundreds of graduate students through their research courses while adding lines to my curriculum vitae. This was not my idea of a meaningful life, and I felt that I was at a crossroads. I knew that this "crisis in meaning" was one that could not be simply solved through becoming better organized, or learning more creative scheduling, or volunteering to be a member on one other committee. I also sensed that the solution to my problem was going to require more of me than cognitive problem-solving or psychological exploration. My spiritual self was in trouble and, thus, a spiritual journey was needed.

So as I rode in the car going home, I began to muse about who I might not be noticing in my own life. Were there souls, or "angels in my path," right now who could assist me in my spiritual search for meaning, connection and purpose? As I asked myself this question, a series of faces drifted across my mind's eye. . . .

Nottoway Correctional Center

Spellman, late 50's, looking angry . . . Andre, 30 something, with a comical expression on his face . . . Saleem, about 40, serious and dignified, but with a twinkle in his eye . . . Carl, early 20's, looking frightened and withdrawn. About a dozen faces entered my conscious-ness one by one, each seemingly with a message that I found impossi-ble to ignore.

These were the faces of a group of men incarcerated in Nottoway Correctional Center, a maximum security prison about an hour away from where I lived and worked. I had met each of them while doing a program evaluation of specialized group services for incarcerated sub-stance abusers. This volunteer program (called the "Inner Child Work-shop Series") had been provided by a woman who volunteered her services to two prisons, one for men and one for women. The work-shop's focus was on understanding how unresolved trauma in child-hood affects one's belief system, emotional reaction, and behavior in later life. I had been contacted by a former student who worked at the women's prison to see if I could help evaluate the program's effective-ness. As a part of the evaluation, I had conducted post-treatment focus groups at each prison to solicit feedback about the program from its participants.

During the group interviews, it became apparent that, although both the men and women found the workshop series as immensely ben-eficial, it had been particularly important to the men. The women, already participating in a therapeutic community within their institu-tion, did not perceive the end of the Inner Child Workshop Series to be a problem. Conversely, these services were unavailable in the men's prison, and they viewed the end of the volunteer program as a major loss. Most echoed the sentiment of one male participant: "I feel like I am finally beginning to understand my life and how I got here, and have some tools to turn myself around, and now the program is ending. I need a lot more."

Deeply touched by what these men talked about in the focus group, I felt conflicted about the ethics of simply "collecting the data," while ignoring the human needs. I decided to help find another volunteer to provide follow-up services for the men, since the original group leader could not continue. However, after several tries, no one had come forth. I struggled with the idea of volunteering but decided it was impossible. I sat in the car with the men's faces hovering around me; I knew I needed to pay closer attention to these souls whose lives intersected with mine and touched my heart—these men had appeared as "angels in my path." I needed to volunteer to do the group for my own sake as well as theirs.

This clarity was soon replaced with numerous "yes, buts. . . ." The prison was so far away—it would take 2 hours just to drive there and back. As a full-time, pre-tenured academic, I didn't have the time; my schedule was unmanageable, and I needed to spend every free moment writing. Doing the group would take up at least half a day or more each week, time I could ill afford. Also, I didn't want to do the group alone; I would need a male co-facilitator, and who would that be? And working with Corrections again! I had worked for 5 years with the department before getting my doctorate and had sworn never to work in that system again. And just who did I think I was? I a middle-aged, middle-class white woman working with a group of African-American men whose lives were radically different from mine? Did I really think it could work?

On the other hand, I felt good about the possibility of putting my whole self where I had been saying my heart was. For several years I had become increasingly concerned about the plight of at-risk kids, particularly young black males. The social and political environment was becoming more threatening to this already vulnerable population. I felt a constant tug to "do something," but rationalized that this work was better left to African-American men who were better equipped to deal with the needs of these children than I was. I began to admit to myself that my reticence had as much, or more, to do with my own fear of rejection than any sensitivity to cultural differences. Here was a chance to be involved in something truly meaningful, and it seemed to be the next step in my spiritual journey.

Three-Child Model of Recovery

I began to grow excited about the possibilities of utilizing a model that my colleague, Dr. Kate Hudgins, and I developed for work with survivors of trauma (Sheridan, in press). This approach, which we call the "Three-Child Model of Recovery," was developed in response to limitations we noted with existing "inner child" models (Bradshaw, 1990; Whitfield, 1986). Briefly, we had observed three problems with previous conceptualizations.

1. When clients attempted to follow messages from their "inner child," they had difficulty in differentiating between healthy, recovery-oriented messages and other internal messages, and therefore sometimes hurting themselves or others.

2. Many clients encountered "inner selves" that were so isolated or severely wounded that they began to see themselves as "damaged or defective goods." In some cases, this reaction developed into a doomed sense about oneself that left the person incapable of mounting the energy needed to do the work of recovery, either because the task was too great or seemed destined to failure.

3. We found that some persons became so stuck in the sadness and rage of earlier trauma that they became unable to take responsibility for themselves and their own recovery. We tried to address these problems through modifying the metaphor of the "inner child" so that its positive role in recovery could be maintained, while hopefully eliminating its unintended negative consequences. We also made a conscious attempt to integrate spirituality into our biopsychosocial understanding of trauma.

Specifically, the Three-Child Model views the traumatized individual as a series of nesting eggs, similar to the Russian carved figures that hold smaller and smaller versions of themselves, one inside the other. The outer egg represents the "adult child;" the physically grown individual who interacts with the world and experiences problems in thinking, feeling, and behaving characteristic of trauma survivors. Below this adult self is another nested egg we labeled the "wounded child." This part of the self is where most of the cognitions, affect, and sensations of prior trauma are held, sometimes partially or wholly unavailable to the adult child. (This was the part of the self that survivors often thought of as their "inner child.") Finally, the deepest nested egg, which we came to call the "sleeping/awakening child," is seen as a patiently waiting spiritual embryo, containing all the positive qualities and life possibilities that the individual possesses. This deeply buried self keeps the seeds of the "true self" or "divine self" safe and protected. Unfortunately, this survival mechanism also keeps knowledge of this part of one's being away from both the individual and others.

This third child state is understood to be the person's spiritual center and the source of spontaneity and creativity or what the father of psychodrama, called the "godhead." Through this part of our being we can experience our own divinity and learn to accept responsibility and co-creation for our lives. Therefore, while the deepest child sleeps, so does our spirituality. Our model suggests that, in persons who are experiencing significant trauma, this core, divine self makes a wise decision

when he or she realizes
that the external envi-
ronment is not going
to provide what is
needed for healthy
growth and devel-
opment. Part of the
self simply goes to sleep, patiently waiting until the
outside world evolves to a point safe enough for
her/him to awaken.

Unfortunately, submersion of this spiritual, core self leaves the "adult child" and "wounded child" to battle it out between themselves, often with negative consequences. The survival tactics of denial, repression, disassociation, and rigid or acting-out behaviors utilized by the "adult child" are not helpful in healing the unresolved issues held within the "wounded child." Conversely, the raw feelings and needs expressed by the "wounded child" often overwhelm the person at the "adult child" level and only serve to convince him or her to utilize old, counterproductive coping strategies even more vigilantly. We discovered that if we helped clients awaken their "sleeping child," or their core, spiritual self, this brought a needed third voice to the conversation, one that could communicate effectively with both the "adult child" and "wounded child." It also seemed to bring the vision, the courage, and the energy needed to do the hard work of recovery at the other two levels. As a result, clients were not as likely to experience the three problems discussed earlier: confusion between healthy and destructive messages, the development of a doomed self-image, and the tendency to become fixed in a victim role.

Most of our work using this model had been with white, middle class adults who had experienced physical, sexual, or emotional abuse. I was anxious to see if the approach could be useful with a different group of people. I knew from the data collected during the program evaluation of the Inner Child Workshop Series that many of the men had reported physical, emotional, and/or sexual abuse in their past. I wondered if the trauma of societal abuse and neglect, which all had experienced, could be effectively addressed using the model, too. Finally, I was interested in integrating a spiritually-sensitive approach to practice that attempted to be culturally sensitive as well. One's racial, ethnic, and cultural background is central to one's identity and sense of place in the world. As African-Americans, I knew that the men at the prison had probably experienced significant wounding of this part of themselves. Thus, any approach, including a psycho-spiritual model such as the Three-Child Model, must consciously recognize, integrate, and honor racial, ethnic, and cultural backgrounds and identities to be both respectful and effective.

The pulls toward working with the group were greater than my fears of doing. And so I decided it would just move forward step by step and trust that, if it were meant to be, the way would be cleared. As the weeks went by, each one of my perceived obstacles fell by the wayside. I applied for and got a University Community Associates Project award that provides released time from teaching one course in order to do community service. A gifted male student, Michael Crosby, agreed to be my co-facilitator as a way of learning more about experiential practice approaches, which I planned to use with the group. He had several years of practice experience in substance abuse and group work and possessed both the strength and gentleness that I thought were needed. An independent study was arranged so that he could receive course credit for his work with the group. Permission from the correctional facility was obtained to run the group, and 17 men were interested in participating. Finally, Tuesday morning was the only time that both Michael and I had free and the institution agreed to let us come at that time. When I expressed amazement at how easily the barriers had evaporated and the way had been cleared, a friend reminded me that "there are no accidents." In any event, whether by a series of lucky breaks or through divine intervention, we were ready to begin!

The following paragraphs provide snapshots of particular group sessions and illustrate the growth in trust and risk-taking that took place over time. Four treatment goals emerged as we worked:

1. Recovery from substance abuse
2. Recovery from previous trauma, both as children and adults
3. Recovery from involvement in criminal behavior, including accepting responsibility and forgiving oneself for harm that had been done to others
4. Recovery from the negative effects of incarceration.

These were the clinical goals, but they were also spiritual goals in that they involved a process of honest self-examination necessary for developing a new vision of oneself and one's purpose in life. I believe that this revisioning is required at various points in all of our lives to recognize and claim our divine nature and unique spiritual journey. Closely tied to these goals was the objective of instilling both hope and pride in oneself as an African-American man. To achieve these outcomes, we endeavored to base our work with the group in cultural and spiritual sensitivity.

● Beginning the Journey

I will never forget when we first stepped into the small room that had been made available for the group. On one side of the room was a door that led directly to a counselor's office that was supposed to be vacant during group time, but was clearly occupied. If we could hear them, that meant that they could hear us. On the other side of the room was a door with a window, which allowed full view of the group by any passersby. Not exactly an ideal environment for developing trust and sharing! In between these two walls was a circle of crowded, disgruntled-looking men. I felt like a timid rabbit needing a safe place to hide. But instead we sat down and tried to begin introductions.

We were immediately interrupted by angry statements that this room would simply not do. One man said he felt like ". . . a sardine packed in this small room." Another said that the "whole institution can hear us through the heat vents. I ain't saying nothin." Others shared similar sentiments. It was clear we had hit our first roadblock. After hearing their concerns, Michael and I agreed that it was a pretty bad situation and that we would try to do something about it. Since we were stuck with it, we asked if we could just use the time to get the group started. With some reluctance, the men agreed, and we began to explain the purpose and expectations of the group. We talked about the group becoming a safe arena for folks to work on the recovery issues identified earlier in the Inner Child Workshop Series. Some looked interested, others looked bored, and all of us looked uncomfortable. I reminded myself that, at this point, all of us were wearing protective masks and that if we just hung in there, our true selves would begin to feel safe enough to come out.

Finally, Michael suggested playing a name game whereby each person would think of an adjective that began with the same letter of his first name. Each person would introduce himself and then introduce all the group members that had come before him to the next man in the circle. Michael started, "I'll begin. I'm 'Manly Mike.' And you are?" With some awkwardness the next man said, "Well, I'm 'Super Sylvester' and this is 'Manly Mike', and you are?" As each man thought up his own nickname and struggled to remember the names of others around the circle, the mood lightened and people started to chuckle—both at the choices of names ("Relaxed Red," "Awkward Andre," "Seeking Saleem," "Sensational Spellman," "Peaceful Paul," "Wasting Wallace," "Friendly Frankie," "Kind Keith," "Attribute Abbey," "Wise William," "Caring Carl," "Learned Lennie," "Researching Rashid," "Messenger Mike,") and the game itself. At the end of the circle, Michael instructed us that we had to go back the other way through all the names. This meant that the first guy, who thought he had to remember Michael's name only, now realized that he had to remember everybody's name. When he pulled off this feat successfully, the group spontaneously applauded and felt as if something important had entered the room through the simple process of naming (and claiming) names.

By the following week, we had secured another group room with much more space and privacy. We obtained it by asking for it. This may not seem remarkable, but in a system characterized by seemingly more barriers than support, it was an amazing accomplishment. The men were impressed and felt as if someone had listened to their needs. I pointed out that the new room had been arranged through the efforts of one of the institutional teachers and the treatment program supervisor. Some stated doubts about any real support coming from anyone who worked there—a theme that appeared many times over the weeks ahead. I noted to myself that our efforts needed to be focused on changing the relationship between the men and some of the institutional staff, as well as on the work of the group itself.

I also reminded myself not to fall into seeing the staff as "the enemy," since that would not be helpful to the group in the long run. I vowed to act from a place of "seeing the light in everyone" when dealing with the staff, as well as the inmates. This approach was hard to pull off sometimes, such as the time we had to wait an incredible amount of time to get through security because somebody couldn't find the right paper work even though we'd been coming in on Tuesday mornings for weeks, but in general it worked quite well—especially when I had to ask permission to do something outside of the usual routine (such as bring in a group birthday cake or a camera to take group pictures or a tape recorder each week in order to play a drumming tape for background music or candles for our closing ceremony). In any event, "mindful respect" served us well both inside and outside of the group.

In that first real session, we talked about how free one could be, or not be OK—physically, emotionally, mentally, and spiritually—inside prison walls. We ended up doing a spectrogram (an experiential technique designed to make internal processes external) to make our discussion more real. One side of the room, near the door, was designated as representing total freedom to be oneself, even while incarcerated. The other side of the room, in the far corner, was targeted as a place where there was no freedom—not to act, to feel, or even to think one's thoughts. I invited the men to place their bodies along the imaginary line between these two extremes and then talk about why they had chosen that particular spot. People took many different places along the line, which surprised me, and spoke quite honestly about their respective positions.

not free

free

At the totally free end, one man said "I feel pretty free in here. I have my routine . . . my job, my studies, and my music. I'm developing my faith here. I choose what I say to whom, but I feel as free to have my thoughts and be who I am in here as I did on the outside. Out there . . . that was not really freedom." At the opposite end, two men expressed how they felt totally controlled. "Man, I think they even control my thoughts sometimes." As the men spoke, I realized that I had assumed that most would choose the "not free" end. I probably had many misguided assumptions and misperceptions about the lives of incarcerated people. I would have to stay open to hearing their truth without preconceived ideas. At this point, the masks were down a bit, and the group was in the process of becoming. Furthermore, the notion that the self may be more than the physical body had been introduced, leaving the way clear to explore our spiritual, as well as corporal selves.

● Unfolding Stories

In the weeks ahead, Michael and I came prepared with specific ideas about what we would focus on during each group and found that we abandoned our plans each week. I learned that I could not predict what would work with this group based on my previous experiences with other client groups. In using the Three-Child Model previously, I usually started with a brief didactic presentation of the model and then moved fairly rapidly to experiential work with each of the child states. I quickly realized that the act of simply talking (about one's ideas, experiences, or feelings) was a major experiential task for these men. Although I could incorporate some psychodramatic techniques fairly easily (such as the spectrogram described above), other techniques such as focusing (a process of guided meditation that facilitates self-awareness and connection with one's spirituality) and role-playing needed slow and needed careful introduction.

Although I was used to working with persons who carried a great deal of pain from previous trauma, generally experienced in their families-of-origin, the level of pain I perceived in these men's lives was more encompassing in that it had been experienced from the larger society as well as within their family systems. In addition, most of the men experienced their incarceration as furthering previous trauma, and worked hard to defend themselves against the pain that came with their current circumstances. We responded by slowing down the process considerably and by letting them lead us to where we needed to go.

Michael and I also directly addressed the issue of racism, which resulted in one of our more productive sessions. During our third session, I asked the men how they felt about doing this group with two white people when all of them were African-American and, on top of that, how did they feel about my being a woman? After some jokes about the desirability of being with a woman for a change, several men started by saying that race didn't matter to them. "You know it doesn't matter to me what color a person is. . . . What matters is whether they're all right or not. You know, can I relate . . . can I trust them? I've known some bad brothers that didn't care that I was black, you know. They did me in anyway."

We spent some time talking about how people are individuals—some good, some bad—regardless of their color. But Michael and I gently pushed the issue and other sentiments began to come out. "Well, I'll tell you. I never trusted any white people, ever. All my life they've tried to mess with me and I don't mind saying that I don't want anything to do with most of them. Now you and Mike, I don't know. I don't know where you're coming from, you know. Why would you two white folk, professionals and all, want to come out here and be with a bunch of inmates? It makes me wonder."

This set off a tense, but honest conversation about negative feelings and experiences that many of the men had with white people and questions that they had about us. Michael and I tried to respond honestly about what we were doing there and stressed that we were getting something important out of being there, that we believed that we would get as much from them as we would give.

To say that the session was uncomfortable at times is an understatement; at one point I was wiping away tears of frustration at feeling that I was being misunderstood by one man in particular. I was trying hard to be honest about my own internalized racism and I felt as if my self-disclosure was being used against me. Other group members rushed in to rescue Mike and me, but we just kept talking, sharing and risking about the very hard topic of race and racism, and the way it affected all of our lives differently. By the end I knew that some of them were afraid we wouldn't come back, but I also knew that we had taken the group to a new level. Because we had the courage to speak our hearts and souls, as well as our minds, a sacred trust had begun to grow among us.

This new level of trust was quite apparent several sessions later when we turned our focus to their lives as children. It was on March 15th—I remember because it was my son's 12th birthday. As I was driving to the institution, I started thinking about the differences between my son's 12 years of life and the men's lives at that age. When I compared the resources, support, and validation my son received from his community and the society at large with the lack of such factors in the lives of many young black men, the meaning of "white privilege" was crystal clear. I was angry about the differences.

With these thoughts in the back of my mind, I started our beginning focusing session with special attention to the men's lives at the important age of 12. They had been growing more and more comfortable with the technique of focusing, and I took a risk that they were ready for some early life work. After helping them turn inward through noticing their breathing and relaxing their bodies, I invited them to go back in time to a younger age—the age of 12, when a young boy becomes a "manchild;" not quite child, not quite grown. I guided them to be curious about themselves at this age and to see if they could notice what this young manchild was like. (Focusing is done slowly with adequate pauses between sentences to allow the person to notice what is true for him/her in that moment.)

"What is he like, this young manchild that was you? Don't push— just notice whatever comes up as you seek to know this young man better. Can you see him or feel him or hear him? Maybe he's just a glimmer. That's fine; just notice what is there and what he has to share with you. See if you can sense how he is physically. Is he growing tall or is he still small? Has his body begun to change? Does his body have a lot of energy, or does he feel tired or weighted down? And how is he feeling inside? What is the expression on his face as you visualize him? What do you think is going on inside of him? Is he happy and proud, or sad or angry? Or maybe he's a little bit scared. What does his heart say to you? Listen. And what about his mind? Is he curious and eager to expand his growing mind? Does he think he's smart? Does he want to know everything there is to know? Has he been told anything about his mind? Good things, bad things . . . And, now his spirit . . . How is it? Can you sense it or feel it—can he? Is it growing along with the rest of him or has something happened to it? How "spirited" is he?

Take him in and see the truth for him, how he really is—physically, emotionally, mentally, spiritually—as he stands in this very special time—this time of 12 years—this time of being a manchild. Now see if there is some way you can make contact with him. . . . You, now a grown man and this child inside of you—this manchild. See if you can catch his eye or pat him on the back or hold him in your lap. Whatever is OK for both of you is fine. And when you're ready, see if you can bring part of him back here, maybe to share with the rest of the group— as much or as little as you want. Take your time, and when you're ready, just let us know you're back by opening your eyes.

When I finished the focusing session, the room remained quiet.

Then one man spoke: "I don't know how in the hell you picked that age—12, I mean. When I was 12, that was some year. . . . Why'd you have to pick that age? I mean, shit . . . I was one messed up little guy when I was 12." He went on to share that he was living with his mom, (his dad had never been with them) and she was tricking for money and drinking heavily and he felt so caught. He was so angry with her and loved her too, and he didn't want to be at home to watch. At about that age, he started hanging more and more with the boys, and the boys all looked up to the men in the big cars, the flashy jewelry, and the wads of money. And he wanted to have someone help him and tell him how to be a man and the drug dealers were the only men that paid attention to him, and so he turned a comer—at the age of 12.

He told his story painfully, with tears and with anger, and the other men leaned their bodies in closer to the circle and lent their support with nods of their heads and respectful silence. One by one, they each talked about how pivotal the age of 12 had been—mostly tales of abandonment from fathers they never knew or stories of physical and emotional abuse from substance-abusing step-fathers or relationships full of negative messages and emotional distance from the few overworked father figures that were still around. And stories of mothers who kept hanging in there—trying to keep the family going and keep their children safe. Or mothers who found their only comfort in bottles or in pouches of white power or in the arms of johns. And one particularly chilling story about the day that belief in goodness and justice and "doing things the right way" was lost when a policeman tried to get a scared 12-year-old to pick up a knife in an alley so the policeman could shoot him as he'd shot "them other niggers."

Everyone had a story to tell. The theme of racism, abuse, and neglect was clear in each account. Racism, abuse, and neglect were imposed by a society that had turned its back on who these young men were and who they could be. Abuse, neglect and negative messages also came from family members living lives of despair and doing the best that they could, but did not understand the effect of the wounds inflicted on their young sons. The spiritual wounding that had occurred to each group member was another theme that rang loud and clear. Instead of being respected and nurtured, the divine child within each boy had been denied and denigrated and "dispirited."

We closed the group session by talking about who those young 12-year-olds were meant to be if they had received the support and nurturing that is every child's birthright. What were their true, spiritual natures? Who were these young children of God? Who would they have become if their circumstances had been different? I watched them as they spoke about what they were like before they learned to hide out within themselves and in the streets—this one's loving nature, another one's zest for adventure, and yet another one's unending curiosity about life around him. Their faces began to light up, and laughter filled the room as they began to grow connected to that true self that had been lost along the way. I knew that the men were beginning to sense their spiritual core—their "sleeping/awakening child" that could help them begin to revise themselves and their lives. As for me, I left the prison that day with a deepened appreciation of my own spiritual child and a joy about her own awakening. This session was a turning point for the group. The level of honesty and the support that we shared that day built a basis for coming together in a different way in the weeks ahead.

The focus of group sessions was diverse. We talked about what it meant to be a man and where those messages had come from. We talked about relationships with women. We talked about maintaining ties with friends and family members on the outside and letting go of relationships that were no longer there for us. We talked about living a life of recovery inside an institution that mirrored life on the streets where drugs and other negative activities are readily available. We talked about how to deal with feelings and how to express frustration and anger constructively instead of falling into the old cycle of perpe-trator and victim. We talked about what spirituality or religion meant to each of us and how we could incorporate it in our everyday lives We talked about learning to trust and open up. We also joked and teased, griped some about the institution's rules, ate cake and cookies, shared talents, waited it out during weeks of lock-down, learned to confront each other's behavior, and came to care a great deal about each other. Far too quickly, the 12 weeks we'd planned came to an end.

● . . . Endings

For our closing session, Michael and I wanted to do a special ceremony to signify the importance of what the group had meant. Unfortunately, when we arrived to begin the group, we were told that since our usual meeting room was being used for other purposes, we'd have to use the staff dining hall instead. This hall is not air-conditioned, and we had to choose between sweltering heat or some relief from a large, noisy fan that drowned out our voices. We chose to live with the heat in order to hear one another. We were also occasionally interrupted by other inmates preparing lunch that day and by correctional officers walking in and out of the area. It reminded me of our first session when the men had complained so about the small, cramped room that we had been given. But this time we simply set about trying to have a meaningful closing ceremony without too much complaint. I had chosen to use the power of a ritual, rooted in both African- and Native-American tradition, to mark the group's ending. On the floor of the dining hall I placed a woven mat of many colors. In the center was a wooden bowl filled with water, a small hand towel, and a large lit candle. Around the edges lay leopard-skin jasper stones from South Africa, which had special meaning to the men given the recent liberation of South Africa. Finally, there were small individual candles for each group member.

One at a time, each group member, including Michael and me, knelt before the bowl of water and the candle and began the ritual. First, each person washed his or her hands in the water while saying, "As a result of this group, I wash away. . . ." One by one we washed away "fear of my own feelings," "hate for all white people," "the belief that I can never get anywhere," "self-doubt and self-hatred," "the need to control everything," and so on.
After drying our hands on the towel, we each selected a jasper stone as a symbol of freedom and as a reminder of the negative thought, feeling, or behavior that we had just released, acknowledging that we would probably have to remember to release it again in the future.

After everyone had his turn at letting go, it came time to claim what each had gained from the group. Again, one by one, each group member took a small candle and lit it from the large candle, which symbolized the power of the group. This time each stated: "As a result of this group, I claim my power to . . ." "give and receive love," "grow in my art," "be a positive force in the world," "turn my life around," "do the work I need to do," "take responsibility for my life." After each statement, the person would join the standing circle, holding his lit candle, while the rest of the group spoke his name and proclaimed: "We honor your power to . . . ," thereby affirming the positive trait that had just been claimed.

At the end, we all stood with sweaty faces and lit candles, oblivious to the noises and stares from persons walking in and out of the room. The group was a group, a sacred trust, and it didn't matter where we were. What mattered was what we had shared and what we had become. Our differences were noted, respected, and celebrated—but our common ties and shared humanity were recognized and honored.

● Transitions . . .

Following this "closing" ceremony, the group decided to continue, although with some changes. My co-facilitator, Michael Crosby, was entering doctoral school and could not continue. My weekly time with the group, provided through the Community Service Associates program, was for one semester, making it impossible for me to continue on a weekly basis. However, I wanted to be with the group in whatever way I could. My initial sense that the men and the group were essential to my own spiritual journey had proven correct. My time with was giving me the sense of meaning and connection that I needed and was fueling the evolution of my own spirit. I was learning to integrate my head, my heart, and my spirit in my work with others, and I was experiencing a sacred human connection. The question was not if I would continue; it was how.

After discussion of various options with the institution, it was clear that our choices were to meet only monthly (when I could find the time to come out) or to meet with another institutional counselor weekly and have me join the group once a month. Given some of the feelings about the institutional staff, it was a real sign of growth that the group chose this latter option. Charles Clay, an institutional counselor, became my new co-facilitator and leads the group during the weeks I cannot attend. It is significant that, after about a month, the men voted to give Charles his own jasper stone as a symbol of his commitment to them and their trust in him.

And so we continue. It's been well over a year since the "12-week" group began. The men have formally named themselves the RESPECT Recovery Group ("respect for self—respect for others—and respect for the community") and we have weathered the transition from the "old" group to the "new" one. A couple of the men dropped out. One man has been paroled and another awaits his release soon. Several men have been transferred to other institutions, which felt like a real wrenching of parts of our soul—but we still count them as part of us. Michael came out to visit during December and will probably come again. And we've developed mechanisms for accepting new members, and have welcomed "Mannered Marvin" and "Victorious Vernon" into our midst. New stories will be shared and our own collective story will evolve.

● Beginnings, Endings and Transitions . . . The Process of Spiritually Sensitive Practice

In working with this special group, I tried to consciously integrate spirituality in four major ways. First, we've purposely talked about it—not a lot, but as an appropriate topic for conversation among many others.

This may not seem like much of a technique or focus, but in much of social work practice, the topics of religion or spirituality are seen as outside of the legitimate realm of social work, and therefore, are considered taboo. I do not talk about it as a religious expert or a spiritual leader or even as a professional with expertise in the area, but rather as one human being to other human beings, all having spiritual parts of self to explore and share with one another.

For example, I've asked the men who are Muslim to explain the meaning and ritual of Ramadan to me so that I could better understand their faith and its importance to them. I've talked with other men about how connected or unconnected they feel to the faith traditions of their childhood and where they are now in their beliefs and practices. We've talked as a whole group about spirituality as one component of the human experience, one that can be attended to and developed just like one's mental, physical, or emotional self. We've also strived as a group not to be judgmental of religious or spiritual differences, but to accept, respect, and support our individual paths.

Second, by teaching the group the "Three Child Model of Recovery," with its explicit reference to the "sleeping/awakening child" state as one's spiritual center, I've also reinforced the spiritual aspect of self as an important focus for exploration and change. As a frame of reference for doing recovery work in many areas, this model communicates the perspective that growth and development are not merely physical or psychological processes, but rather an enterprise best approached holistically. It is important to utilize processes that emphasize a sense of purpose and meaning and connection, as well as cognitive, affective, and behavioral change. Furthermore, the model suggests that the spiritual core of self provides the vision and energy for doing the hard work at other levels. For example, when the men discovered and shared the true nature and potentialities inherent in their 12-year-old "manchild" selves, they started to regain a vision of self that had been lost and, hopefully, found some of the energy needed to recapture and redirect that vision.

Third, many of the techniques or approaches that we've used in the group have a spiritual component. The very act of "focusing," for example, is a process for turning inward for the purpose of gaining deeper knowledge about one's core self. This process of deeper connection with self usually leads to more meaningful connections with others and often with a life force beyond oneself—whether that life force is known as God or Allah or the Great Spirit or the Goddess or the mystery or the power of the group. Other specific exercises helped group members to focus on where they were developmentally in terms of spiritual, as well as physical, mental, and emotional growth. And the use of ritual, as in our "closing" ceremony, directly brought a sense of the sacred into our human interaction and provided both meaning and symbolic memory for future endeavors.

Fourth, the frame of reference I've employed in entering into my work with the group and my relationships with the men—initially and before every group session, recognizes the spiritual nature of the work itself. At the very beginning, as I rode home from the movies, I asked a prayerful question of myself and the universe: "Who am I ignoring that I should be paying attention to?" The answer was immediate and clear, as the pictures of the men at Nottoway began to parade before my eyes. During a time when I was searching for meaning and purpose in my personal and professional life, the group emerged as a sacred experience that has furthered my own spiritual path.

As such, I try to utilize one of the methods of "holistic prayer" that Canda (1990) describes in his discussion of the many approaches to prayer that can be appropriately utilized in spiritually sensitive practice. I try to take the time to prepare myself before each meeting with the group, to picture and think about each individual, to ask for guidance and support in my interactions with them, to thank the Mystery for the opportunity to be with them, and to center myself so that I can be wholly present and genuine during our time together. Sometimes the hectic reality of my life results in my spiritual preparation being less than I would like. But at all times, I view my work and my relationships with these men as a gift—one that graces my life and one that I hope enhances theirs.

This combination of a conscious, nonjudgmental focus, a therapeutic model that includes spirituality, the use of spiritually based techniques, and a recognition of the spiritual nature of the work itself all blend together into "spiritually sensitive practice." It is certainly not the only model of such practice, but it works for me with this group of men at this time. It will certainly evolve and change as we do, and I look forward to the new experiences and lessons that lie ahead.

● Postscript: The Many Faces of Angels

As I was writing this narrative, I received a letter from one of the men from the group. He asked me if I had ever seen a television show on Saturday night about an angel, and he went on to say that it reminded him of me. My first knee-jerk response was to caution him quickly not to put me up on some kind of pedestal, as I certainly was no angel—and I did ask him not to be idealistic about me when I wrote him back. But as I later realized, and included in the letter, we all have the capacity to be angels to one another, and so I thanked him for the compliment. I also told him that I had seen the "glimmer of his own wings" in group a time or two. I, for one, am grateful that I noticed the "angels in my path" and am very, very glad that I paid attention.

● References

Bradshaw, J. (1990). *Homecoming: Reclaiming and championing your inner child.* New York: Bantam Books.

Canda, E. R. (1990). An holistic approach to prayer for social work practice. *Social Thought, 16*(3), 3–13.

Sheridan, M. J. (in press). Individual experiential therapy: The Three-Child Model of Recovery. In K. Hudgins (Ed.), *Healing sexual trauma: An experiential practice approach.* New York: Guilford Publications.

Whitfield, C. L. (1986). *Healing the child within: Discovery and recovery for adult children.* Pompano, Beach, FL: Health Communications.

● Reflective Inquiry

1. What is your view of the "psycho-spiritual model" used by Sheridan in her work with males incarcerated in prison? Explain.

2. What do you think made it possible for this white woman (Sheridan) to engage in spiritual sensitive work with the group of African American incarcerated men?

3. Have you ever been in a total institution such as a prison, a hospital, the military, a religious order? What are your thoughts and feelings about those experiences as you remember them?

Making the Past Meaningful: Kwanzaa and the Concept of Sankofa

by Maulana Karenga

The African American holiday of Kwanzaa has become an important cultural practice among millions of African American peoples throughout world African community. This is a narrative of the process of conceptualizing and institutionalizing Kwanzaa, and its vision and values as expressed in the core values of Kwanzaa, the Nguzo Saba.

The creation of the holiday Kwanzaa is rooted in and reflective of the 1960's liberation movement, the conception of my role as an activist-scholar, and the vanguard role of my organization Us as a cultural nationalist structure dedicated to creating, re-creating, and circulating African culture and the struggle for a just and good society.

As an activist-scholar in the 1960's, I had felt a profound need to use my knowledge in the service of the people, and make it available to the masses to improve and enrich their lives. This commitment to serve came from the life and lessons of great men and women I admired and studied, and from the lessons and expectations of people from my childhood. Our mother and father, our immediate and extended family, our friends, our public school teachers, and the sheltering ancient oaks we called "old folks" and "elders" all expected and predicted that I would do something of lasting value to serve our people and honor our family.

With this in mind, in 1965 I left the University of California, Los Angeles, and the doctoral program in political science with a specialization in African Studies. I began to organize and teach in the community, sharing my knowledge, shaping circumstances, and searching after what would be good for the future. My activities expanded after the Watts Revolt of 1965, a turning point in the Movement and a point of departure for my involvement in "the struggle."

I had worked in the civil rights movement earlier, demonstrating against chain-stores with segregation policies in the South, and assisting in fundraising, rallies, and forums on and off campus on the meaning and goals of the struggle. The Revolt became a sign and symbol for the need to turn inward, establish community control, acquire, and practice what came to be called Black Power. I defined the goals of the Black Power Movement as a collective thrust to achieve and maintain three things:

1. Self-determination (freedom in the general sense and community control in a specific sense)
2. Self-respect (self-understanding and self-appreciation rooted in paradigms from our own culture)
3. Self-defense (the collective capacity to end existing oppression and abuse, and prevent future oppression and abuse by the state, especially by the police).

The urgency of this project was underlined by the assassination and sacrifice of Malcolm X, and the models of liberation by African countries. The Revolt illuminated and framed the issues in the discourse of power. The central message was that students like me had a special obligation to work on the project as we were more idealistic, less economically vulnerable, and less restrained by the demands of daily life. We agreed that we must dare to struggle, win, and build the new moral community we wanted to live in.

To do my work and to achieve something of lasting value, I created two basic instruments: an organization called Us and a theory called Kawaida. The name *Us* was chosen to indicate two things: the communitarian views, values, and practice of the organization, and our commitment to us as a people distinct from them, the rulers of the established order. Kawaida, in Swahili means tradition, but in the context of its theory, it refers to an ongoing synthesis of tradition and reason directed toward cultural grounding and social change. Within this framework I conceived the project of Kwanzaa and enumerated the Nguzo Saba, (The Seven Principles) that form the core of its conception and practice.

From 1965 on, the expression and process of the Movement was essentially Black Power. One of its central tenets was the need to "return to the source," to get "Back to Black," in a word, to return to all things African, especially the most important things. The focus was on recovery, reconstructing African culture, reappropriating it, and reaffirming it as a living tradition. In this context cultural practices such as renaming oneself and one's children with African names; wearing the natural or Afro hair style and African clothes such as the buba, kanga and dashiki; relearning and learning African languages, especially Swahili; and reinstituting African life-cycle ceremonies such as naming (Kutaja jina), nationalization (Akika), wedding (Arusi), and passing (Maziko), were or are being developed.

● Re-Africanization

Within this thrust for re-Africanization, Black Studies was established in the academy, and the network of community institutions to restore and reinforce African culture was expanded. These institutions included cultural centers, independent schools, theaters, art galleries, and brotherhood and sisterhood formations. Re-Africanization also involved a return to Africa itself for cultural and spiritual revitalization, and the reestablishment of mutually beneficial relationships and exchanges. At the core of this commitment to re-Africanization was the attempt to recover and recommit oneself to learning and living African values as an indispensable way to rebuild and reinforce family, community, and culture. Kwanzaa as an institutionalized cultural practice serves as a central way of reappropriating and reaffirming African culture.

I moved to this position and became a leader of this movement for several reasons.

1. The civil rights struggle had revealed the weaknesses of ideas about assimilation. Certainly, we all wanted desegregation, but I and others rejected integration. Desegregation would destroy barriers to the exercise of rights and free exchange, but integration, as I

read it, assumed that we as persons and a people wanted and needed to be with whites to achieve and fulfill ourselves. This I rejected of necessity.

2. I began to conclude that cultural pluralism was the best way to achieve quality relationships and mutually beneficial and cooperative exchanges in society. I had championed cultural pluralism in a letter to the editor in 1960 in the *Daily Collegian* at Los Angeles Community College. Then, my position was a liberal cultural pluralist one. Now I advocated a cultural nationalist pluralism.

3. I emphasized re-Africanization because I perceived that cultural identity was the most fundamental way to understand and realize oneself. One's concept of humanity is inescapably tied to the cultural paradigms. As an African, I chose to understand and realize myself in and through African culture.

I embraced this position with greater fervor when I discovered the rich, varied, and ancient character of African culture. As an intellectual, I had been surfeited with and turned off by the Eurocentric approach to human knowledge. It seemed at one point that all subjects taught were openly or surreptitiously long and boring self-congratulatory narratives of Europe and European peoples. I needed to know and understand my culture and the cultures of other peoples of color, but especially my own. So, I detached myself from schools and the circles of associates and friends from the civil rights movement and turned inward and toward Africa. I found, in both continental and diasporan African cultures, models of human achievement and human possibility that informed my conception of self, the good life, and the just, good society. Within this context I began my process of re-Africanization, returning to my own history and culture and building structures and processes to achieve and spread my views.

Role of Us

My organization Us formed the vanguard in the re-Africanization process. Us argued that culture is the key crisis and challenge in Black life. Moreover, Us maintained that the crisis is solved and the challenge met by self-consciously overturning oneself, by institution-building and by the social struggle which reshapes persons, and culture, and aids in the creation of a just and good society. Us linked the improvement and enrichment of African American life to the rescue and reconstruction of its culture and the struggle to reshape, reappropriate, and create a new society.

This position was argued within movement organizations. Some organizations argued for strength through education, others for economic development, and still others for "picking up the gun." We maintained that all these ways were necessary but not sufficient because what was needed, as Fanon said, was a total solution on the objective as well as the subjective level. Such a solution required culture, i.e., the totality of thought and practice of a people. We concluded that we could find guns anywhere, especially in the hands of the oppressor. What was necessary was for the people themselves to decide that struggle itself is necessary and then determine and develop their means. Thus, we argued for a cultural revolution to create a new logic and language of liberation and new institutions to house and advance our aspirations.

Kawaida Theory

We understand that the stress on culture would justify itself if it were inclusive enough to deal with the demands of daily life and struggle. Therefore, Kawaida theory defined culture in its fullest sense as the totality of thought and practice by which a people creates itself, celebrates, sustains and develops itself, and introduces itself to history and humanity. It occurs at least in seven fundamental areas: history, religion (spirituality and ethics), social organization, economic organization, political organization, creative production (art, music, literature, dance), and ethos, i.e., the collective psychology which results from practice in the other six areas of culture.

Kawaida maintains that the quality of social practice is directly related to the quality of the cultural views and values which inform and ground it. Values are defined as categories of commitment and priorities which enhance or diminish human possibilities. What one considers important and places first in one's life determines the quality and direction of one's life with both persons and peoples.

These assumptions about culture and values led me to study African cultures and ask what was the social cement that held these societies together and gave them their humanistic character? Moreover, how could I make these ancient traditions live again? How could I use and teach others to use the past to inform and give foundation to the present and future? How could I use the lessons of the past to move effectively in the history we now live?

My conclusion was that the core of humanistic African culture is its communitarian values, values which reaffirm and reinforce community and human flourishing. The challenge was to assemble a set of communitarian values which reflected both the best of African tradition and modern ethical reasoning to establish a core set of values for the African community. Moreover, they had to be values that spoke to the needs of the community and the demands of the struggle—values that would enhance the people's sense of identity, purpose, and direction and support their efforts to live free, full, and meaningful lives. Such a set of values would have to have be conceptually elastic to allow for rich and varied interpretations to accommodate the diversity of thought and practice of African peoples, and represent a core value system that could be easily grasped and learned because of its manageable number and meaningful focus and message.

Sankofa, an Akan concept of historical recovery, literally means "return and retrieve it," but conceptually is more expansive. It requires a recovery, the result of intellectually rigorous, culturally grounded and future-focused research. What I wanted to do was not simply extract from the past but to discover and recover values that pose models of human excellence and suggest paradigms of human possibility. The practice of Sankofa requires constant dialog with African culture. A central self-understanding of Kawaida is that it seeks answers to the fundamental concerns of the African and human community to define the best of what it means to be both African and human.

This dialog was conducted inside Us and with other African groups, institutions, and scholars, and in public and community forums with the masses. The central dialog was inside Us, for recovery and reconstruction of African culture and its use in enriching and expanding our lives as our central mission. Therefore, the struggle was not simply to defeat our oppressor, but to imagine a new way of being human, and new paradigms of human relations and human society to bring into being. Paradigms of possibility for Us resided in the ancient and varied richness of African culture. In this context I conceived and put forth the Nguzo Saba (The Seven Principles) as a core Black value system which reaffirms and reinforces family, community and culture. I developed Kwanzaa as a fundamental way to introduce, institutionalize, and spread these principles. Kawaida theory and the Nguzo Saba gave form and substance to

Kwanzaa, making it a fundamental mode of cultural recovery and recon-struction.

● The Inception of Kwanzaa

Kwanzaa was created first as a fundamental way to rescue and recon-struct African culture in the midst of a movement for re-Africanization. It was to recover a valuable and ancient way of building family and community, shaped so it spoke to current needs and aspirations as a paradigm of possibility. Second, I created it to introduce the Nguzo Saba (The Seven Principles) and to reaffirm the centrality of commu-nitarian values in building and reaffirming family, community and cul-ture. Kwanzaa was also created to serve as a regular communal celebration which reaffirmed and reinforced the bonds between us as African people both nationally and internationally. And finally, Kwan-zaa was created as an act of self-determination as a distinct way of being African in the world. It was conceived as a cultural project, as a way to speak a special African truth to the world by recovering lost models and memory, reviving suppressed principles and practices of African culture, and putting them in the service of the struggle for lib-eration and ever higher levels of human life.

The first celebration in 1966 was essentially an organizational cel-ebration with guests and friends of Us. It set the pattern for subsequent celebrations which I outlined in a typed paper and sent around the country to other nationalist organizations. The process included ingath-ering, rituals thanksgiving; remembrance and recommitment; and cele-brations of the good. As an intellectual, I was always concerned with laying groundwork and setting forth a clear and definite framework, but I was equally concerned with allowing flexibility for developmental change as distinct from destructive change. In 1966, I put forth the basic framework and content of the Kwanzaa celebration. It anticipated and allowed for changes that reaffirmed its basic principles and lessons, and enriched and expanded celebrants' understanding, appreciation, and practice of the holiday.

As Kwanzaa developed, I continuously stressed the need for think-ing and talking about Kwanzaa as a way to reaffirm and reinforce fam-ily, community and culture. This way of approaching Kwanzaa as reaffirmation and reinforcement serves at least two purposes. First, it does not deny strengths African peoples already have but stresses the ongoing need to expand on these. As Nkrumah says, we must "go to the people; start with what they know and build on what they have." Thus, Kwanzaa seeks to reaffirm and reinforce the internal strengths of the people by emphasizing communitarian life-affirming, struggle-supporting and achievement-encouraging values which come from our own culture.

Second, to stress Kwanzaa's drawing and building on the best of our culture is to reaffirm the need to protect and expand it. If we respect African culture and above all African people, we must struggle to create the context in which both can flourish. While the vision, values, and practice of community strengthen the people, their own struggle will liberate them and lay the basis for a just and good society.

The Seven Principles

I posed the core values of Kwanzaa, the Nguzo Saba, as a system, a set of moral values by which the African community could reconstruct our lives in our own image and interests and pose a critical model of family, community, and culture. These Seven Principles are:

1. Umoja (Unity)—to strive for and maintain unity in the family, community, nation, and race, i.e., the world African community
2. Kujichagulia (Self-Determination)—to define ourselves, name ourselves, create for ourselves, and speak for ourselves instead of being defined, named for, and spoken for by others; as the ancient Egyptians taught, to think with our own mind, feel with our own heart, see with our own eyes, hear with our own ears, speak with our own mouth and walk with the strength and dignity of our own person
3. Ujima (Collective Work and Responsibility)—to build and maintain our community together and make our sisters' and brothers' problems our problems and to solve them together
4. Ujamaa (Cooperative Economics)—to build and maintain our own stores, shops, and other businesses and to profit from them together—to share work and wealth, and build and control the economy of our community
5. Nia (Purpose)—to make our collective vocation the building and developing of our community in order to restore our people to their historical greatness
6. Kuumba (Creativity)—to do always as much as we can in the way we can to leave our community more beautiful and beneficial than we inherited it

7. Imani (Faith)—to believe with all our heart in our people, our parents, our teachers, our leaders, and the righteousness and victory of our struggle—faith in ourselves, in our Creator, in our mothers and fathers, our sisters and brothers, our grandfathers and grandmothers, our elders, our youth, our future and faith in all that makes us beautiful and strong. We need faith in the righteousness and victory of our cause, faith that through hard work, long struggle, and a whole lot of love and understanding, we can and will self-consciously step back on the stage of human history as a free, proud, and productive people.

I used Swahili because it is the most widespread African language and thus represented the Pan-African character of my political and cultural vision. For this same reason, my organization Us had introduced Swahili as the African language of the Movement and fostered its use in language classes; in naming persons, organizations, and buildings; and in greetings and useful phrases.

I constructed the order of the principles to start with Umoja (Unity) and to end with Imani (Faith). I started with Umoja (Unity) because there is no family, community, or culture without unity. It is, of necessity, the beginning and continuing need. But then come questions of unity for what, around what values and practices, and how to achieve unity in thought and practice? The other principles help explain the nature, purpose, and practice of unity—unity for and through Kujichagulia (Self-Determination), and unity directed toward community and African self-determination in the cultural, economic, and political sense. It is a unity for and in freedom which is, in fact, the practice of self-determination, in and through community. Unity, in turn, requires Ujima (Collective Work and Responsibility). This teaching of ancient Egypt says that the good done for others is good we, in fact, do for ourselves. In doing good, we are building the moral community we, ourselves, want to live in.

We also commit to Ujama, the principle and practice of cooperative economics through shared work and wealth. Ujama makes all beneficiaries and bearers of responsibility, reinforces cooperative values, and lays the basis for cooperative projects. Moreover, establishing national purpose (Nia) and reassessing and redefining it constantly is an imperative. This national purpose becomes our collective vocation as a people. It is important that it is always informed by our best moral vision and values. There is the challenge to always be creative, to act like the Creator, to constantly bring into being the good and the beautiful, and to strive to leave our community better and more beautiful than when we inherited it. This is the principle of Kuumba.

Finally, Imani (faith) is the principle from which all principles are drawn. We require faith in ourselves and each other to constantly practice. Thus, we say, let us all and each have profound and continuing faith. We can and will return to our own history and self-consciously step back on the stage of human history as a free, proud, and productive people.

Kwanzaa, like all other holidays, requires symbols. The symbols, like the holiday itself, represent a synthesis of tradition and reason, ancient practice and modern engagement, and continental African culture and African American culture. In choosing symbols, I was concerned with cultural authenticity and relevance for the present and the future.

Certainly, being in the midst of an historical struggle for freedom would have to be reflected in both the symbols and their interpretation. Moreover, the symbols had to reflect not only the demands of struggle, but reaffirm and reinforce the best of our cultural values. These would begin with the values and symbols of communitarian and first-fruit celebrations of which Kwanzaa was an expression.

The Symbols

Kwanzaa has seven basic symbols and two supplementary symbols. These traditional and modern symbols evolved out of the life and struggle of African American people. These basic seven symbols are:

1. Mazao (crops)
2. Mkeka (mat)
3. Kinara (the candle holder)
4. Muhindi (corn)
5. Zawadi (gifts)
6. Kikombe cha umoja (the unity cup)
7. Mishumaa saba (the seven candies).

The two supplementary symbols are a poster or other representation of the Nguzo Saba (The Seven Principles) and the bendera ya taifa (the national flag or standard).

The first symbol, the mazao (crops), represents the historical roots of the holiday itself and the rewards of collective productive labor. The concept of Kwanzaa as a first-fruit celebration has its roots in the communal agricultural celebrations of continental African peoples.

Mkeka (mat), the symbol of tradition and history, is the foundation for correct knowledge and understanding of self, society, and the world. Therefore, all other Kwanzaa symbols are placed on the mkeka, and it too becomes a foundation. The kinara (candle holder) is symbolic of our parent people, the continental Africans, our ancestors as a collective whole, both the African man and the African woman. The muhindi (corn) represents children and all the hopes and challenges attached to them. Zawadi (gifts) are symbolic of the seeds sown by the children (i.e., commitments made and kept) and of the fruits of the labor of the parents.

Kikombe (the unity cup), or its full name—kikombe cha umoj a—serves two basic functions. First, it is used to pour tambiko or libation for the ancestors, and second, it is the ritual drinking cup to reinforce unity in the family and community. The mishumaa saba or seven candles represent The Seven Principles which are the heart and spirit of Kwanzaa. The candles are placed securely in the kinara, the symbol of ancestry, to symbolize the rootedness of the ancestral principles. The lighting of the candles is a daily ritual during Kwanzaa which symbolizes giving both light and life to the principles themselves and raising up light to lessen darkness in both the spiritual and intellectual sense, an ancient African concept. As the Husia, the sacred text of ancient Egypt says, "I have driven away darkness so that light could be lifted up."

Two supplementary symbols are the Nguzo Saba and the bendera. The bendera are the Black, Red, and Green colors given to us by the Hon. Marcus Garvey. In the 1960's we reordered the colors and slightly adjusted their interpretation to correspond to our current needs. Thus, we said the colors are Black for the people, Red for our continuing struggle, and Green for the future we shall build out of struggle.

The Fundamental Activities

Kwanzaa is organized around five fundamental kinds of activities which reflect both its origin in the practice of first-fruit celebrations and its rootedness in communitarian values. Regardless of differences in language, name, and cultural location, Kwanzaa and other first-fruit celebrations revolve around these common activities. First of all, Kwanzaa is a time of ingathering of the people. It is a time to come together and reinforce the bonds between us as a people in spite of our diversity. Thus, Africans who are Muslim, Christian, Jew (Hebrew); followers of the ancient African traditions of Yoruba, Maat, Dogon, Ashanti, Dinka, and other religious traditions celebrate Kwanzaa. It is a cultural holiday, not a religious one. African culture is diverse and the home of innumerable religious traditions. Old and young reach across generations and embrace and find in Kwanzaa a common ground of heritage and promise. It is a special time for calling home all family members, reaching out of friends and neighbors as well as the community at large and reinforcing the bonds of family, community, and culture. And so all are urged to reach out; reconcile and re-embrace each other; forget differences and celebrate commonality as family, community, and culture; and to enjoy the goodness of peaceful togetherness.

Kwanzaa is a special time for reverence for the Creator and the creation. Therefore, its observance emphasizes spiritual grounding; rejoicing, and giving thanks for the gift of life, thanks for our families, our community; and our culture and the promise of our future. Because it is based on ancient African harvest celebrations, it is also a time for giving thanks for and committing ourselves to respect for nature, its beauty and bountifulness. The agricultural and harvest focus of the holiday gives an excellent context for special appreciation of nature and the universe and concern for the continued health of the earth; natural abundance; and our right relationship with the Creator, humans and nature. The ancient Egyptians and other African peoples teach that the Divine, human and natural, are linked; that harm to one is harm to all; and that good done to one must and does include good done for all. Thus, African people remember and meditate on this, teach it, and cultivate the principle and practice of right relationships with the Divine, human and natural.

Kwanzaa is a special time of commemoration of the past. It provides an excellent context for teaching and celebrating the most ancient history and culture in the world—African history and culture. We remember Fannie Lou Hamer's statement that there are two things we must all care about, "never to forget where we came from and always praise the bridges that carried us over." And thus we embrace Kwanzaa, a special time to teach the rich beauty of our history and to praise the great bridges who carried us over—Harriet Tubman, Frederick

Douglass, Mary M. Bethune, Malcolm X, Ida B. Wells, Martin L. King, Anna J. Cooper, Marcus Garvey, and others. We also praise the small and sturdy bridges who did not make the history books, wear kente cloth or speak an African language, but still taught us African values by teaching us to dare to struggle, speak truth, do justice, and walk in the way of righteousness.

As a people conscious of our culture, we know both the meaning and value of memory, the moral obligation to raise and remember those who gave their lives, love, and labor so that we might live fuller, freer, and more meaningful lives. And we teach these to our families and community and honor the ancestors by living their best and most beautiful lessons. Moreover, we take seriously the obligation given us in the teachings of Mary McLeod Bethune, who said, "We are heirs and custodians of a great legacy," and we must bear the burden and glory of that legacy with strength, dignity and determination.

Kwanzaa is a time of recommitment to our highest ideals. It is a time of focusing on thought and practice of our highest cultural vision and values which in essence are ethical values—values of love, sisterhood, brotherhood, and respect for the transcendent, the human person, for elders, and nature. There the Nguzo Saba (The Seven Principles) serve as the central focus of Kwanzaa. These communitarian values are both cultural and ethical and enrich our lives as such.

We are, in the final analysis, defined by our values and the practice to which they lead. Thus, Kwanzaa teaches us to remember and act on the ancient African teachings of Maat which say, "Speak truth, do justice and walk in the way of righteousness." The Husia says we must always show preference for the most vulnerable among us, "give food to the hungry, water to the thirsty, clothes to the naked and a boat to those without one." We must be "a father to the orphan, a husband to the widow, comfort to the sick and a staff of support for the aged, a shelter to the needy, a float for the drowning and a ladder for those trapped in the pit (of despair)."

In this special time of recommitment to our highest ideals, Kwanzaa is especially a time of sober assessment. The major day for this is on the last day of Kwanzaa, January first, but all through the holiday one is challenged to think about what it means to be African. Those rooted in African culture reaffirm that, above all, being African is being culturally and ethically grounded. Being committed to culture and its ethical core that teaches us to struggle for liberation constantly and ever higher levels of human life, to speak truth, do justice, love rightness, serve the people and realize that "every day is a donation to eternity and even one hour is a contribution to the future."

We embrace Kwanzaa as a time to ourselves and to ask members of our families and others three basic questions which Frantz Fanon says we all have to ask and answer. They are: "Who am I?" "Am I really who I am?" and "Am I all I ought to be?" "Who am I?" is a question of identity. It reminds us we are an African people—fathers and mothers of humanity and human civilization who taught the world in the midst of Nile Valley civilization some of the basic disciplines of human knowledge, sons and daughters of the Holocaust of Enslavement, and authors and heirs of the Reaffirmation of the Sixties. The question, "Am I really who I am?" is a question of authenticity, realness, genuineness. It reminds us not to mask our Africanness, distort our appearance, deny the rich and varied beauty of our people, or do anything that damages our inherent human dignity or demeans our history as an African person and people.

The last question, "Am I all I ought to be?" is a question of ethical and historical obligation. It reminds us that as an African people who are fathers and mothers of human civilization, we must always strive for the highest level of achievement; that as sons and daughters of the Holocaust of Enslavement, we must oppose all forms of human oppression—especially racism, sexism, classism; all forms of enslavement, external and internal; and we must remember and honor the millions lost by completing their struggle for freedom and by living the full and meaningful lives they intended for us.

And finally, as authors and heirs of the Reaffirmation of the 1960's, we must not let our oppressor be our teacher; we must create and put forth, out of our own understanding of our history and culture, a new paradigm of what it means to be human, of human relations, and of the just and good multicultural society.

Kwanzaa is a time for celebration of the good, the good of life, family, community, culture, friendship, the bountifulness of the earth, the wonder of the universe, the elderly, the young, the human person in general, our history, our struggle for liberation and ever higher levels of human life. Celebration is a ceremony, commemoration, a respectful marking, an honoring, a praising and a rejoicing. This and more is our holiday of Kwanzaa, ancient and modern thought and practice, a joyful achievement and an ongoing and unending promise.

Activities must be collective, cultural, and reaffirming and always honor the dignity of our people and culture. The celebration of our history and struggle, our ancestors, our love, the awesome beauty of nature, the promise of life, and the achievement of hard work, are of necessity called forth. Men and women who are rooted in their culture model and mirror the best of what it means to be African, and build a beautiful and beneficial future. They know that every word and act must teach and help us to move effectively in the history we are now living. These persons of culture know that Kwanzaa is part of that living history and rich tradition and play a vital role in celebrating and reaffirming the legacy of our history and the promise of our future.

● Growth of Kwanzaa

Each year has seen the further growth of the holiday of Kwanzaa with an estimated 18 million African people celebrating it throughout the world African community. It is growing among African people in the U.S., Africa, Brazil and other countries of South America, Canada, the Caribbean, and Britain and other European countries. Last year it began in India.

The question is always raised, "Why does it grow among African people?" The answer, of course, lies in how it speaks to them; serves their needs; and points to ways of celebrating, and reinforcing family, community and culture. In fact, as I have so often stated, Kwanzaa is growing among African people because it speaks to their need and appreciation for its cultural vision and life-affirming values, values which celebrate and reinforce family, community, and culture. It is growing because it represents an important way Africans speak their own special cultural truth in a multicultural world. It is growing because it reaffirms a rich and ancient tradition which lays claim to the first religious, ethical, and scientific texts and the introduction of some of the basic disciplines of human knowledge in the Nile Valley. It is growing because it reinforces our rootedness in our own culture in a rich and meaningful way. And it is growing because it brings us together from all countries, all religious traditions, all classes, all ages and generations, and all political persuasions the common ground of our Africanness in all its historical and current diversity and unity.

When I see the growth of Kwanzaa and its rootedness among African people, I am obviously pleased. It is clearly a celebration which millions embrace as a cultural legacy of significant and lasting value. Therefore, it has become a work which contributes both to my self-definition and my self-understanding. Moreover, it stands as a central part of my overall work as an activist-scholar; my development of Kawaida theory and building the organization Us out of which Kwanzaa emerges; my work in the cooperative founding and development of Black Studies, including contributions to the concept of Afrocentricity and my pioneering work in ancient Egyptian ethical philosophy as a critical field in African Studies; my general Sankofa project of historical recovery and reconstruction as expressed in the development of rites of passage programs and other life-cycle rituals; the creation of the Simba Youth Movement as a model of possibility and promise; my political organizing and activities in and of Black united fronts and national leadership formations; and finally, my development of the Nguzo Saba which are used as a fundamental theoretical and value orientation in literally hundreds of organizations around the country.

Certainly, I feel fortunate, even blessed, to see my work established and flourishing in my lifetime. For so many who deserved this did not see it. And yet I am always conscious of the fact that there is still so much more to do, because as the ancestors taught, "it is good to work for the future," because the "good we do for others we are actually doing for ourselves" and because "every day is a donation to eternity and even one hour is a contribution to the future."

● Bibliography

Asante, Molefi. (1987) *The Afrocentric idea,* Philadelphia: Temple University.

Asante, Molefi. (1990) *Kemet, Afrocentricity and knowledge,* Trenton, NJ: Africa World Press.

Carmichael, Stokely and Charles Hamilton. (1967) Black Power: *The politics of liberation,* New York: Random House.

Carson, Claybourne. (1981) *In struggle.* Cambridge, MA: Harvard University Press.

Drewal, Henry J., John Pemberton III and Rowland Abiodun. (1989) Yoruba: *Nine centuries of African art and thought.* New York: Center for African Art.

Evanzz, Karl. (1992) *The Judas factor: The plot to kill Malcolm X.* New York: Thunder Mouth Press.

Fanon, Frantz. (1967) *Black skin, White masks.* New York: Grove Press.

Frankfort, Henri. (1948) *Kingship and the Gods.* Chicago: University of Chicago Press.

Gendzier, Irene. (1973) *Frantz Fanon: A critical study.* New York: Pantheon Books.

Gyekye, Kwame. (1987) *An essay on African philosophical thought: The Akan conceptual scheme.* New York: Cambridge University Press.

Karenga, Maulana. (1989) *The African American holiday of Kwanzaa: A celebration of family, community and culture.* University of Sankore Press.

Karenga, Maulana. (1976) *Afro-American Nationalism: An alternative analysis.* Unpublished dissertation. United States International University, San Diego.

Karenga, Maulana. (1990a) *The book of comingforth by day: The ethics of the declarations of innocence.* Los Angeles: University of Sankore Press.

Karenga, Maulana. (1988) Black Studies and the problematic of paradigm: The philosophical dimension. *Journal of Black Studies,* 18, 4 (June).

Karenga, Maulana. (1993) *Introduction to Black studies.* Los Angeles: University of Sankore Press.

Karenga, Maulana. (1980) *Kawaida theory: An introductory outline.* Los Angeles: University of Sankore Press.

Karenga, Maulana. (1986) *Kemet and the African world view.* Los Angeles, University of Sankore Press.

Karenga, Maulana. (1977) Kwanzaa: *origin, concepts, practice.* Los Angeles: Kawaida Publications.

Karenga, Maulana. (1994) *Maat, the moral ideal in ancient Egypt: A study in classical African ethics.* Unpublished dissertation, University of Southern California, Los Angeles.

Karenga, Maulana. (1990b) *Reconstructing Kemetic culture: Papers, perspectives, projects.* Los Angeles: University of Sankore Press.

Karenga, Maulana. (1984) *Selections from the Husia: Sacred wisdom of ancient Egypt.* Los Angeles: University of Sankore Press.

Malcolm X. (1965) *The autobiography of Malcolm X.* New York: Grove Press.

Menkiti, Ifeanyi. (1984) Person and community in African traditional thought. In Richard Wright (ed.), African Philosophy, Washington, D.C.: University Press of America.

Morenz, Siegfried. (1984) *Egyptian religion.* Ithaca: Cornell University.

National Education Association. (1974) *The legacy of Mary McLeod Bethune.* Washington, D.C.: NEA.

Niangoran-Bouah, G. (1984) *The Akan world of gold weights: Abstract design weights.* Volume I, Abidjan, Ivory Coast: Les Nouvelles Editions Africaines.

Nyerere, Julius. (1969) *Freedom and Socialism/Uhuru na Ujamaa,.* New York: Oxford University Press.

Pinkney, Alphonso. (1976) *Red, back andgreen: Black nationalism in the U.S.* New York: Cambridge University Press.

Toure, Sekou. (1958) *Toward full re-Africanization.* Paris: Presence Africaine.

Williams, Juan. (1987) *Eyes on the prize.* New York: Viking Press.

● Reflective Inquiry

1. What is your opinion about the creation of Kwanzaa?

2. Dr. Karenga in proposing Kwanzaa, made the analysis that cultural pluralism was the best way to achieve quality relationships and mutual beneficial cooperative exchanges in society. What is your view of his proposal?

3. Kwanzaa's core values emphasize: (Umojaa): to strive and maintain unity in the family; (Kujichagulia) self determination: (Ujima): collective work and responsibiity; (Ujama): cooperative economics; (Nia): national purpose/and the process of redefining and reassessing; (Kuumba) creativity, bring in the good and the beautiful; and (Imani): Faith. Compare these values to those of one of your spiritual/cultural holidays.

5

Spirituality in Faith

by Sarah Sloan Kreutziger

The author worked with seriously-ill patients in a hospital setting in the 1970s. This chapter recounts some stories of the connections between her spiritual perspective and the relationships and activities with patients.

Bob was a physician in the state-run university hospital in north central Florida that employed us both during the decade of the 1970s. He asked if his wife Sherry could interview me about a psychology project she was doing on religion in the workplace. I was flattered since Bob and I often kidded each other about our respective religious beliefs. On more than one occasion, he told me that I would make a good member of his non-trinitarian denomination if I could just give up "that Jesus thing." I agreed that he was probably right and also agreed with Sherry's request to look at how I used my religious faith in my medical social work practice.

Sherry was a bright and energetic researcher. I answered general questions about my religious background and training. We were doing well, I thought, until I innocently told Sherry that, while I did not actually pray with my clients, there were times when I said silent prayers before and after the sessions, as well as when we seemed to be "stuck." I mentioned a recent case where a woman had dragged her very reluctant husband in for counseling for a rapidly failing marriage because of his new relationship with another woman. He was adamant that he wanted out of the marital relationship as soon as possible. I admitted that even I was surprised that after I said a silent prayer for guidance, he suddenly made a 180 degree shift and agreed to further counseling. Sherry had no trouble understanding my implication that God had heard my plea for help.

But Sherry was not impressed with my magical thinking. Her facial expression and negative tone of voice reinforced her barely concealed disdain as she grilled me relentlessly until I shrank under her reprobation. I began to feel somewhat desperate and told her about research at Duke Medical Center by Dr. William Wilson (Wilson and Jones, 1978), a psychiatrist, on the efficacy of prayer with psychotherapy patients—all to no avail. In her mind's eye, it seemed, I had eliminated myself from all claims of professionalism by exemplifying the stereotypical version of an evangelical religionist: hopelessly irrational, unredeemed even by my liberal-humanist training. To her, I seemed to be a "True Believer" (Hoffer, 1951) in the sense of fanaticism, doing god-knows-what damage to my helpless clients.

In at least one respect, Sherry had assessed me correctly. I am a "heart" more than a "head" person. I am a member of the United Methodist Church, a religious tradition which has historically been known for its "people of the warmed heart." Like Hillary Rodham Clinton (Woodward, 1994, p. 23), my faith was honed on the legacy of the Social Gospel, or what John Wesley had earlier called, "practical divinity." This is the call to act on behalf of others in response to God's unrelenting love and action in our own lives. I couldn't explain this to Sherry because her own sense of professionalism appeared to be wedded to an empirically based agnosticism that precluded openness to even gentle metaphysical intervention in therapeutic practice. Nor could I explain this to her husband because it is all connected in my soul with "that Jesus thing."

I had tried for a while to ignore "my Jesus thing." I went into social work because it allowed me "to save the world" as a secular missionary during a long period in early adulthood as I rotated among cycles of agnosticism/atheism/agnosticism. As a young student, I had eagerly embraced the new god, Freud. I embraced the Methodism of psychoanalytic theory as the newer way to human perfection. I believed his prediction in "The Future of an Illusion," i. e., that religion would disappear as humankind relinquishes this harmful illusion in favor of progressive scientific knowledge

(Freud, 1961). 1 worked diligently as my professors urged me to remove all traces of my middle-class morality and to become value-neutral in the fight to save humankind by objective and scientific methods. I spent time in confession with my supervisor repenting of careless remarks to clients that betrayed my misguided beginnings in the morality of my childhood. She duly recorded my misdoings in my evaluations, which served as a kind of absolution by humiliation. And I dutifully filtered my thoughts and words to reflect these new doctrines.

To this day, I'm not sure when my belief in this newfound knowledge began to falter and become hopelessly entangled with my older religious beliefs. I suspect that it occurred when I had children. Having children made it more important for me to forge connections between my past and future. Probably a large part of it occurred, however, because I was a lousy atheist in one significant way: I couldn't quit going to church. Despite my best efforts to disengage, I still loved the feel of church: the rituals, the symbolism, the music, the people, the fellowship, the shared values, "the going onto perfection." In short, I loved the connection with the community, the symphony of good people doing good works. There the *Hound of Heaven* (Thompson, 1986) found me and howled until its peace made a place within my soul.

This positive connection to church became reinforced in my work. As a beginning social worker, I found myself relieved, for example, when I discovered that my dialysis patients were heavily involved in their churches, especially those patients from rural communities. I knew from experience that support systems would likely be formed to feed the family, to comfort them, and in many cases, to work to raise money for the 20% costs of treatment not covered under Medicare.

● The Case of Dean

One of my first cases involved such a person. Dean, an unmarried, white, 19 year old, was the first person in his very supportive family to graduate from high school. His father was a hard-working, barely literate farmer who tried diligently to understand his son's medical condition even if he could not understand the psychological pain of being an adolescent hooked three times a week to a dialysis machine. He brought his son regularly and never gave up hope that somehow Dean would recover and realize his potential.

Unfortunately, the attending doctor had not seen Dean's potential in quite the same way. In fact, Dean was deemed to have a mental disability and therefore (this was the early 1970s) unfit for the limited resources of our unit. Because, however, the small community, under the leadership of a determined lay woman from their Pentecostal church, had so rallied around the family with almost monthly fund-raisers and corresponding publicity, I could make the claim that the family had the financial resources and emotional support to go on dialysis. A hospital committee agreed; thus the young man was treated for two years until his death after a failed transplant from an older sister. This interval gave the other medical personnel time to know and care for this family as much as I did.

My recognition of and comfort with the language of religious belief had also enabled me to work with the family and church community before and after Dean's death. I had already discovered that families were often reluctant to talk with professionals about spiritual matters because of their astuteness regarding the invisible barriers signaled by professionals uncomfortable with this area. As a result, I had tried to become an open and friendly oasis in an unexpected place by being sensitive to the signs of subtle forays into this forbidden zone. I found that simple affirmation, merely a positive nod in agreement with religious claims, created an atmosphere conducive to exploring the benefits of a religious ideology that builds on the strength of positive belief.

Over and over again, I discovered that the patients were openly relieved to find someone to share their very real fears and the existential questions that come in moments of personal crisis. I learned to listen with new ears to the familiar language of the heart as people reached out in hope and prayer for the miracle of healing, or at least for the miracle of understanding and acceptance. And in that familiarity, I was allowed to share the deeper levels of their experiences and to learn from their courage and strength. My clients became my teachers and 1, in turn, shared their lessons with the others who would follow me.

● The Case of Mike

Of course, these lessons were forced upon me time and time again. On one occasion I worked with a 32-year-old, married, African-American blacksmith named Mike whose diabetes had, over the past four years, made him blind, impotent, and disabled with the loss of one leg.

Although Mike had grown up in a devout Baptist family, his desire to work while he was still able crowded out his previous church-going activities. This caused him to relegate religious concerns to the shadows of his mind. There they stayed, surfacing briefly through his other medical setbacks and emerging full blown when kidney failure forced him into a long hospitalization.

He became understandably depressed, and he and I spent many hours reminiscing about his past in preparation for an uncertain future. In a long session when we were exploring the existential questions of his fate in terms of ultimate justice and mercy, I over-stepped my bounds with a glib apologetic about God's will in relation to his predicament. I explained to Mike that although God's ways are often inscrutable, I was sure that he was not being punished for past sins as he supposed.

In retrospect, I realize that in my eagerness to defend God, I had not listened to what Mike was really saying and had brushed aside a major coping mechanism: bargaining with God. In other words, in Mike's world view, if he could seek God's forgiveness, then God might lift the punishment of devastating illness, or at least lessen his suffering.

Fortunately, Mike paid no attention to me until I called in our hospital chaplain, who was able to offer realistic comfort (and absolution) through the ascribed power and authority of his sacred position. From that time on, the chaplain and I worked as a team, with mutual consultation and concern about the patients who requested spiritual guidance.

● The Case of Mrs. S

Sometimes, even acceptance and openness to religious language and issues were not helpful in working with patients. Mrs. S., an elderly Jewish woman, had tested the patience of every staff member with her incessant demands, including one that all of us working with her belong to her religious culture and tradition. When she was referred to me, she objected strenuously because I was outside her faith. However, she softened a bit when the resources I was able to secure on her behalf made her stay more comfortable. Still, she continued to complain until I told her (truthfully) that one of my ancestors *may* have been Jewish. At that moment she relaxed, told me that she suspected this all along, and worked amicably with me from that point on. Had I not had that ancestor, I suspect that she would have still worked with me, but not as quickly or as happily.

● Near-Death Experiences

Another man, an elderly writer named Mr. G., at the end stage of a devastating form of cancer, faced his death with a proud atheistic stance despite the incessant pleas of his family to return to the comfort of their Reform Judaism. After I was able to secure his trust by respecting his decision, my work focused on helping the family accept it as well. Because they knew that I, too, would have been happy for Mr. G. to reverse his decision, we were able to talk candidly about their disappointment and grief balanced with his right to self-determination. Since Mr. G.'s atheism was characteristic of a life-long pattern of self-mastery and control, his behavior was easier for them to accept when we discussed it in the context of Mr. G.'s strength of personality and his integrity. He could apply this strength toward dying as he had lived.

In the remaining two weeks of his life, Mr. G., his wife, his two grown children, and I shifted the focus of the discussions into memories of pleasant times together and the beliefs and values that they shared in common. Mrs. G. never fully gave up hope that Mr. G. would change, but he died with his unconquerable soul intact. I prefer to believe, how ever, that he had a surprise waiting at death.

The surprise I'm referring to comes out of the research on neardeath experiences that was a consequence of my work with seriously ill patients. Early in my career, I discovered that, despite close and frequent contact with my patients, in almost every case, I had not seen them for at least three weeks before they died. When I realized this avoidance, I was forced to face my own fears of death. I still held tremendous guilt, for example, that I had avoided Dean as his health declined, at a time when he needed me and others the most.

In an effort to deal with these fears and failures, I attended a workshop given by Dr. Elizabeth Kubler-Ross, author of several books and one of the pioneers in the Death Education Movement. Dr. Kubler-Ross mentioned research done by Dr. Raymond Moody, who at that time had not yet published his best-seller, *Life After Life* (Moody, 1976). I wrote to Dr. Moody and attended one of his workshops. With a fellow-church-member cardiologist, I began some of the very early research in that area, using some of the experiences of my patients who had quietly hidden these episodes from us until we asked (Sabom and Kreutziger, 1977).

While this work did not prove that there is life after death (for me such a belief is still in the realm of faith), it did show that for many people the experience of death is a peaceful and painless experience. It also fit into my spiritual belief that a Benevolent Power ("that Jesus thing" again) would be there in the bad times as well as the good. This offered a comfort that could be shared with those nearer to death at that time than I. Since there was a tremendous amount of publicity about the study then, patients sought me out for this information, which I offered only at their request and to the extent that they were interested. To some it gave immense relief; to others it was too mysterious and alien. But for me it offered enough peace about death to calm my fears. From that moment on, I was present with my patients until their ends, and I connected with their families for many months, sometimes years, beyond.

● Misuses of Spirituality

Of course, as the allegorical tale of Lucifer tells us, everything God-given and therefore good has the potential for misuse and destruction. Opening ourselves up to the spiritual realm of our patients' lives also opens up the dangers this can bring and the pitfall we must watch for. I suspect that this is often the reason social welfare professionals shy away from exploring the transpersonal values of their clients/ patients. Several of my cases raised important questions about the misuse of spirituality and the challenge of responding appropriately for healthy refraining and healing.

One of my continuing challenges came from patients or clients who understood enough of my religious tradition to trample upon its good intent in socially dysfunctional ways. The husband of a seriously ill patient, for instance, enlisted my help in getting churches and other charities to donate money for his wife's care, which he really used to feed his drug habit. In another case, a recovered cardiac patient wanted my help in applying for social security benefits. In such situations, the dilemma for me was how to establish appropriate boundaries with these individuals when my religious values stressed uncondi-tional love and service.

This dilemma actually was the easiest to resolve since Christian belief also stresses accountability for one's actions as part of our covenant with the Creator in response to all empowering grace. I believe that as temporary stewards of the creation, all of us, worker and client together, are obliged to hold all gifts, including the gift of love extended in service, in sacred trust until these gifts are returned to their Source. Speaking this truth from a stance of "tough love" was part of my vocabulary long before I read, "The worker who does not permit the client to exploit him [sic] and who scrupulously makes clear that he [sic] will not settle for the superficial has a good chance of engaging the client in an active identification process" (Zentner, 1984, p. 258). Committed religionists have long known that "cheap grace," i.e., love without cost or fixing limits (Bonhoeffer, 1963), prohibits building strong helping relationships with individuals just as it prohibits building strong societies.

Another challenge I faced in the realm of working within the context of religious commitment arose from the dilemma of helping people to stay connected with religious supports even when they might expose clients to harm. For example, a woman with a mental disturbance, who was connected to her church's supportive network, attempted suicide after misinterpreting a sermon urging sacrifice of one's life so that others (interpreted as her ill daughter) might live. Mrs. M., a white, 39-year-old, married housewife was an active member of a small church whose theology stressed rigid accountability to biblically based codes of behavior and adherence to reified doctrines about sin and salvation. She was close to members of her congregation and sought the advice of her minister. She fought off physical exhaustion and depression while she took care of her 17-year-old daughter, who had a debilitating illness. The minister and the other members of her church visited her regularly after her hospitalization for her attempted suicide. The psychiatrist and I decided to make him a part of the treatment effort since he seemed eager to help and was somewhat embarrassed about the unintended consequences of his preaching. He wanted to make sure, as did we, that Mrs. M. didn't attempt suicide again. Since Mrs. M. was far more willing to listen to him than to us, we were able to enlist his help in interpreting and reinforcing beneficial therapeutic interventions in Mrs. M.'s life by a mutual examination of the causes and dynamics of a psychotic depression. After several weeks, Mrs. M. was released after a very successful recovery. The continued follow-up and consultation between and her minister provided important monitoring and support for her.

Bill, a 42-year-old, white, married businessman, who was being evaluated as a potential transplant donor for his sister, presented another problem in terms of diagnosis and treatment. He spent over an hour during a very intense initial visit trying to convert me to his evangelical view of Christianity which had saved him, he said, from a life of alcoholism. After I finally told him that I was already in the fold, he relented enough to allow me to continue the interview. In my report, I interpreted his rigid traits as a warning sign of a personality that I felt was loosely integrated and held in precarious balance only by the strong, structured tenets of his religion. However, I was the single person on the medical-psychiatric team to note any concerns. Since Bill turned out to be the only eligible donor, the decision was made to go ahead with the transplant.

Right before the operation, Bill had a psychotic break, making my words prophetic. My diagnostic ability had been greatly enhanced, I believe, because Bill had sensed my openness to his religious views. He did not hold them in check as he had with other interviewers, allowing me a glimpse of his character and its vulnerabilities. Fortunately, after several months of psychiatric treatment, which he was willing to undergo in order to help his sister get well, the transplant was successfully completed.

Perhaps the greatest ethical challenge for me arises from the gap between the psycho-medical environment and possibly misguided religious beliefs. For example, I was challenged by patients or families who refuse life-saving medical care because of their religious values. As a Christian, I believe in spontaneous healing and the power to control one's medical destiny in limited ways, but I also believe that healing comes through traditional medical methods as well. Sometimes, reframing the situation in such a way encouraged immediate cooperation. However, my experience has been that time and process play larger roles in cases where the final decision is made to accept standard medical care. Obviously, patients also have the right to refuse treatment, but they usually do so before they reach the hospital. Sometimes, the patient's change of heart occurs when the medical symptoms become too obvious to be denied, and other times it occurs when these individuals are introduced to others who share their experiences and therefore understand their doubts, concerns, and fears.

In one such case, an acquaintance named Lynn, who knew of my hospital experience and religious commitment, invited me to her home to share her holistic spiritual beliefs and values as context for her argument for miraculous healing. She gave many examples of how her organic, vegetarian diet and meditative methods made her 15-year-old daughter Susan, who had serious kidney disease, feel better. I listened, explained as much as I could about others' experiences with renal failure (including the dietary need for protein), prayed with her at her request, and then asked her to meet with another friend named Mary who had gone through the same experience with a child suffering from end-stage kidney disease. She did.

Some weeks later, when I checked on the progress of the helping relationship, Mary admitted that she had lost contact, but agreed to call Lynn and see her again. When she did, Lynn's daughter was so critically ill that they both took her to the hospital. When the doctor refused to treat Susan unless it was done in the medically approved manner, Lynn relented and allowed Susan to be dialyzed. Susan did well, eventually received a transplant, and had a very successful recovery. Lynn now attributes Susan's remarkable progress to the power of prayer and the community's support. Lynn, in effect, did her own reframing.

In a sense, Lynn's story is symbolic of what happened to me and others who choose to share the journey of faith of seriously ill patients. We start with our own sense of truth, enter into relationships with others whose difficult situations force us to face with them some of life's most challenging questions, and reframe our beliefs and values based on what we hammer out within those interactions. This process occurs in the context of what theologian Paul Tillich (1963) called "the eternal now." Seriously ill individuals and those who love them often do not have time for abstract philosophical meandering along existential pathways, no matter how alluring. They are confronted with a direct threat to their temporal future. They force those who care about them to confront that threat as well. They need all the resources available to them, including ones that offer spiritual comfort and solace.

● The Rewards

For those who accept the challenge to walk the more narrow path with them, and who do not shun their religious beliefs and values, the rewards are enormous. My patients and clients helped me to refine skills I had learned in Sunday School. They taught me to listen to the silence of thoughts too profound to express. They taught me how to respond carefully to the quiet of these meditations. I learned that words have great power for healing if used wisely and potential for great harm when they are not. I learned that just being with Dean or Mike or Lynn was often as important as anything I could do tangibly. "The evidence of things not seen" is a powerful corollary for any treatment derived from science.

My patients forced me to confront my own existential anxieties in order to help them face theirs. I had to move beyond time my youth and inexperience and wobbly religious faith in order to fortify my practice and knowledge for their benefit. I had to leave behind romantic and shallow notions about what it meant to face major disability and the possibility of death as those with whom I worked allowed me insight into their private struggles and suffering. I had to acknowledge my own reluctance to give up the fight to keep my patients from giving in to the inevitable when they had clearly signaled that they were ready to do so. I had to risk exposure to values and beliefs far different from those I had grown up with and to respect the integrity of their right to coexist with mine. Most of all, I had to learn to support the courage that comes from staying the course minute by minute, day by day, just as the accumulated wisdom of my religion teaches me to do.

The growth process was emotionally and physically exhausting, but it helped me define the limits of my strength in ways that still serve me. I've learned to wait in order to let each situation unfold enough so that I can clearly respond to the realistic needs and desires revealed, rather than to my own compulsion to do something. I've learned to appreciate the strength of support systems for recovery, both for the patients and their families and for those of us who work on their behalf. I've learned to prioritize by separating the wheat from the chaff in the context of the gift of each new day that comes without any guarantee of another. I've learned to take to renew my spirit through worship, music, prayer, and play.

Each renewal of these lessons recaptures the memory of the serendipity of those earlier experiences. I use the memories as part of practice wisdom to pass on to the students whom I now teach. Whether

I consciously realized it at the time or not, the learning that my patients and I forged together, undergirded by my religious faith and values, emphasized the healthy aspects of behavior and belief, long before words such "empowerment" and "working with the client's strengths" became fashionable. I owe my patients much.

● References

Bonhoeffer, D. (1963). *The cost of discipleship.* New York: MacMillan.

Freud, S. (1961). *The future of an illusion.* New York: W.W. Norton & Company.

Hoffer, E., (1951). *The true believer.* New York: Harper & Row Publishers, Inc.

Moody, A. (1975). *Life after life.* Georgia: Mockingbird Books.

Sabom, M.B. & Kreutziger, S.S. (1977). Near-death experiences. *Journal of the Florida Medical Association,* 64 (Sept.), 648-650.

Thompson, F. (1986). The hound of Heaven. In M.H. Abrams (Ed.), *Norton Anthology of English Literature* Vol. II (pp. 709-14). New York: W.W. Norton.

Tillich, P. (1963). *The eternal now.* New York: Charles Scribner's Sons.

Wilson, W.P. & Jones, E.D. (1978). Therapeutic prayer. *The Bulletin,* 4 (1),35-38.

Woodward, K.L. (1994, October 31). Soulful matters. *Newsweek,* pp. 23-25.

Zentner, M. (1984). Antisocial personalities. In Turner, F.J. (Ed.), *Adult Psychopathology* (pp. 345-363). New York: The Free Press.

● Reflective Inquiry

1. How do you describe your own development in the context of social work—spirituality? Closer to Sherry, to the author, or an other perspective?

2. The author explains she had overstepped her bounds with a patient because

   a. she was not listening and had brushed aside (his) a major coping mechanism: bargaining with God; and

   b. told a patient she had an ancestor who was of the same religion.

   What do you think of the way the worker dealt with both situations, and what might you have done?

3. Can you imagine yourself working with Lynn and doing what the worker did? What do you think of the author's explanation? that "Lynn's story is symbolic of what happened to me and others who share the journey of faith of seriously ill patients."

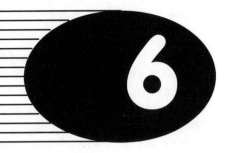

American Indian Narratives: "My Spirit is Starting to Come Back"

by Christine T. Lowery

American Indian women have a concept of relationship that extends across time and to all living things. They come from similar places and use those places to solidify relationships with one another.

When I first saw May, I saw her in a way that tugged on my memory, sensing something familiar but having no proof of how I knew her. May, a woman from the Yakama tribe in Washington, was the first of six women I interviewed in a study of Indian women and their addiction and recovery processes. I used the life history to gather data and to explore her life with her in a series of interviews. As a researcher, I did not anticipate May's themes of grandmother and granddaughter and foster child to braid into the themes in my own life as a Laguna/Hopi (Pueblo) woman and Indian child welfare worker. But it should be no surprise, for as Indian women, our lives in middle age are not the reflection of ourselves in a mirror, but the reflection of our relationships through the generations.

To help is to share strength that continues to influence us over time. May and I share a larger connection in our research relationship, a trust that permits memories that come from the experiences of our people to be relived and, in that reliving, to be reinforced for the truth and comfort they represented the first time. It was in the stories of May's experiences of abuse in child welfare that I connected with her most strongly. These stories reignited my role of protector as an Indian child welfare worker. I will tell you these stories in four circles, circles that intersect time and cross generations: recognition, child welfare, "my spirit is staring to come back," and coming home.

● The First Circle: Recognition

In 1993 when I interviewed May, she was 52. In our culture, May was becoming an elder, a teacher, a leader. May had double bypass heart surgery at 49, and the scars of surgery crisscrossed her chest. At 50, she was working out a seven-year relationship with her lesbian partner, who was in her sixth year of struggling with sobriety. That same year, May had a bout with pneumonia and won, despite her weakened physical condition. When she was 51, AIDS hit her gay and lesbian community with force, and the couple lost many friends. After 28 years of alcoholism, at age 52, May had 12 years of sobriety. She had finished 10 years of working in the alcohol field and received her certification for chemical dependency intervention. She was diagnosed with diabetes that year. Her social service agency had been notified of pending budget cuts, and she and some of her co-workers faced possible unemployment.

My connection to May is intergenerational. She is a large woman, dark skinned, broad shouldered, barrel chested, with a face that marks hard time. I saw my own Laguna grandma somewhere in her face, the way I must have seen my grandma when I was a little girl. Interestingly, May recognized me, too. In 1993, 1 was seven years younger than she was, and May was the age my grandma would have been when I was born.

"I've gotten a lot better about just staying within my own little . . . sober world," May says in the fourth interview, "and it's growing and there's a lot of people that are coming in, like you. You're coming into my circle and my world and I find that I'm not hesitant or ashamed to talk about some real personal things. I don't know you," she adds.

"I know!" I exclaim.

". . . Yeah, and that says a lot about . . . your being able to present trust and my being able to accept it," she continues.

"This is the one thing that has amazed me," I start. "And I mentioned this to one woman [I was interviewing], and I said, 'You know, you don't know me. I'm literally off the street.' And I'm walking in . . ."

"But you're a native woman," May interrupts.

"I know!" I whisper. "How much of a difference does that make?"

"I would probably be real . . . ah . . . veiled in some of my responses," May begins. "I'd have real cliche," she pauses, "because I am a con, and I know how to do that kind of stuff. And I've done that before to people who are asking questions. They're very glib answers and very pat and stir all the passion in that person . . . but I didn't have to do that with you. Because for some reason I've seen you before . . . you know. You've been there before, somewhere; you've been there and I recognize you. Nobody would understand that if they weren't native."

"Which is why," I respond, "when I see you, I see a Pueblo woman."

"Uh-huh," she answers, nodding her head.

"And you look, . . . you look familiar to me too," I say. "In fact when I came up [the steps tonight] I recognized your profile . . . and you do . . . you . . ." I wanted to tell her she looked like my Laguna grandma but May was ahead of me.

"Because I can go to [your] country and they come up and start talking to me like, 'Yeah, where's your family?' you know. 'Well, they're from Washington State.' 'No you're not!' I have this image that fits a lot of tribes . . . and it's amazing how it works."

May stops, she is thinking, then she continues the circle of her thought: "Not that there wouldn't be a lot of people that I would talk [to] about my alcohol history. Because I've had students who tried to interview me and they're very intrusive. Now, I've told you stuff that I'd never tell anybody, but that wasn't intrusive for me because you allowed me a lot of freedom. Their [questions were] really structured and they always have a way of letting you know, 'that-isn't-the-right-answer.' They look at you, so then you stop.

But you're still pleasant and you're still kind and you never change the expression in your voice, but 'Well that's about it,' you know. . . . Because they want the right answer, they don't want the truth. They want the right answer. And that's totally different between Indians and non-Indians. And it's so sad . . . but it's real because that's how they talk to us. I get real tired of people who always go, 'Oh . . . you're so spiritual.' And I'm just like, 'Ri-i-ight.' I worked real hard to even find anything spiritual. Because I didn't know what that meant. I thought it meant religion, just like they did."

May continues: "One of the things I couldn't understand in terms of recovery was, they talked about a spiritual program and, . . . and words like 'God' . . . and what I thought [was] religion. And [understanding what spirituality was] didn't happen for me until two years into my sobriety, when my mother died. I had not been formally trained as a young woman in the culture that follows certain traditions, follows certain protocols when it came to a death in the family. But all of a sudden all of those things just came to me. I knew where she was to be buried. I knew the name of the place. I knew the name of the cemetery, I remembered where it was. And I knew who to hire to do the dressing service and the [funeral] service and knowing I had to find a gatherer [to gather berries and roots] and what I needed to do in terms of hiring cooks and hunters and fishermen and it just went boom, boom, boom.

"And I had not been formally trained so it felt like, 'okay. I have a spirit that's telling me in my spiritual part.' And I wasn't thinking in terms of God. I was thinking in terms of maybe a creator, or I don't know, but it was there. It felt really good. It kind of gave me some comfort to know that I was doing the things that I needed to know how to do, as the eldest [woman] now. And it was my place to take care of all of this. My brothers had nothing to do with it because I was the one that's supposed to do this. And I did it. And the old people came to me and told me, 'Yes. Yes.' I didn't have to stand around and not know what to do. And all of a sudden people started turning toward that part of me to take care of other things that might go on like an illness or whatever."

● The Second Circle: Child Welfare

May's history is one of separation and attempted reconnection, a pattern common for many Indian youth in her generation and the generation before and the generations that follow. Before she was five, she spent some time with an elderly maternal great aunt and uncle, grandparents from an Indian perspective. Eventually her grandmother went blind. May vaguely remembers that she might have been sexually molested by a grandfather but doesn't really remember. Could this be why May was removed from her grandmother's home at age six and placed in a Christian mission boarding school? Or was it her grandmother's blindness?

She only remembers that she was never allowed to go home, carried away in a common practice that pre-dated by 32 years the Indian Child Welfare Act of 1978, legislation designed to keep Indian families together. May would be placed in a series of foster homes all within a hundred miles of her family and her tribe, but May would not see her grandmother again. May did not see her mother again until she was 21 and pregnant with her first child.

"They just came in and said they were going to take me, and they did. I don't remember the story or anything. I remember one day I was at my grandma's and the next day I was there. And I never saw my grandmother again."

When May was taken away at age six, she was ill most of that first year away from home. Mumps, measles, and whooping cough swept through the common living quarters of the Indian children at the Yakama Indian Christian Mission.

May sighs as she begins her story. "It was the First Christian Church that sponsored it. All the little girls stayed in one end of the building and the boys stayed somewhere else. We went to a public school and they would hit us every time we'd try to talk our language. The principal would hit us with flash cards if we talked and . . . he was always hollering at us out on the playground if we talked. And I couldn't understand where everybody was, like my mom and every-body, my grandma. And I really hated going back and forth on the buses [from the mission to the public school in town].

"From there I went to town the beginning of my second grade [to live with Mrs. King, the 55-year-old matron of the boarding mission]. And I was the only Indian in *that* school so I got a lot of name calling. There were a few kids who were nice to me; they seemed to be the ones that went to the church that Mrs. King went to. She made me get bap-tized at eight. And she would say, when she would beat me up, she would say, 'We're going to take that heathen out of you, that evil out of you.'

"But the hardest part was when people would tell me that I was dirty or I wasn't as clean as them 'cause, 'Look at you!' I'd look and all I could see was the brown and they had white skin. So I'd go wash and wash and wash. Then when I was in [another placement] my sixth grade year the same thing went on . . . the feeling I always had to go into the school prepared to take somebody's stuff that day. It was usually the boys . . . and then the girls would say it too. And so I usually ended up just going off by myself. So I did a lot of daydreaming and . . . wishing for things. I'd read the signs on the cars at the car lot and they'd say 1995, and I'd count my dollars. And I'd count 19 dollars," May laughs, "and 95 cents and that's not what they meant, you know. But I thought as a kid, if I can buy one, then I can go home. But I never did ever get one so . . . I always was able to be by myself and I could do things alone.

"I used to envy people being white because they always got everything. And no one necessarily called them names unless they really looked different, were like funny or something, then people would call them names."

"Do you think if you were in another place, not in . . . those small little towns, you would've been treated differently as an Indian person?" I ask.

May was not part of an Indian family that had prestige, and she had mixed blood, Yakama, Quinault, mixed German and French. "I was a breed. And my mother was with . . . a black man. There was that element of [she sighs] prejudice. "I don't know if I would've been treated differently . . . if I'd been in another city or a bigger town. . . . All I know is that during that time I learned how not to like leftovers, because I always ate when everybody got done, especially through the 6th to 9th grade . . . I was always the outsider and everybody was telling me how grateful I should be because they let me live there. You know, I should show more respect for these people because, after all, they took me in.

"But nobody would talk to me about all the [foster care] checks they took either . . . nobody mentioned that. And I was the one that went to jail, not Mrs. King . . . when I ran away when I was in 5th grade. . . . Later I went back with Mrs. Baker, my caseworker, to pick up my clothes and . . . nothing was mentioned about [the abuse]. Mrs. Baker was just this cheery. I thought, 'Geez. Why don't you go in there and punch her out or something, you know.' know I'd get beat almost every week."

May was removed from Mrs. King's and placed in another home. "[This] time they treated me fairly decent in terms of not beating me up," May says. "But I was 12 and I took care of Donna who was two and they called the baby Baby June, who was like eight months or something. And I took care of cleaning the house and doing those things. And mealtimes, I ate leftovers. I ate what was left on the table.

But I had to hurry and eat real fast because then I had to do the dishes. And I had to have them done before a certain time."

"You didn't eat with the family?" I ask.

"No," says May.

When I heard these stories, I was catapulted into my social work practice as a child welfare worker on a reservation. In the mid-80s, a group of five children were in our care and I interviewed a childless Indian couple that was willing to serve as foster parents for all five children, in shifts. The first two children, ages 18 months and 3, were placed in the couple's small, two-bedroom apartment. Later, when the couple was able to rent a large trailer with multiple bedrooms, the other three siblings, ages 4, 5, and 6 were placed.

I was the original caseworker and, over the course of a year, talked with the birth mother of the children about the sexual abuse experienced by the 5- and 6-year old girls. I talked with the mother's sisters and their mother about the future of these children. None of the relatives was able to care for the children; the patterns of drinking and drug abuse continued in this generation, as they had in the last. And the sisters agreed that they were unlikely to change their habits while the children were still small. The mother came in and talked with the couple, who had decided, by then, that they could adopt and raise these children. Eventually, the mother relinquished her rights.

In the meantime, the school-age children were being seen by the school psychologist. The new family was seen by a contracted team of white therapists who specialized in treating sexually abused children and who worked with the foster parents as well. The children had a new Indian social worker who was monitoring the case and I was completing the adoption study.

Here was a model case, an Indian child welfare agency with 80 percent Indian staff, working with an Indian foster/adoptive home, good therapy resources. The formal adoption would go before the tribal court in six months. So when the oldest child was taken to the emergency room after being beaten by the foster father, we were all in shock. When the child told about the sexual abuse by the foster father, we were sick.

Bad things happen to children even in foster care and even under watchful eyes. Hindsight unmasked the red flags that could now be seen by the therapists. "She drew pictures about someone watching them while they took showers, but we thought it was when they were in the home of their biological mother." "Ah yes," said the non-Indian group home director sanctimoniously, "The wife bears all the symptoms of a battered-woman."

And as I listened to May tell her story, I reviewed my own role as protector. In my heart I held the young May in my lap and I rocked her, just as I had rocked the child who had been beaten: "I am so sorry. We're the ones who are supposed to watch out for you, to protect you, and this should have never happened." And the seven-year-old raised her hand and wiped my tears away.

● The Third Circle: ". . . my spirit is starting to come back"

"Zero to five years old is when we learn all our values and our morals and it's from our environment and it's . . . set in us" May says. "And no matter what else transpires, no matter what else happens, that hope, you asked me about, somewhere in there, in those first five years there was some hope that it didn't have to be the way it was. . . . In those first five years I was with my grandma, and she taught me a lot of things about . . . living and being, being nurtured and being cared for. I don't remember my grandmother hugging me or kissing me or anything, but I knew she was always there. And she would always protect me.

"So I'd find myself . . . slipping back, going through my turmoil and chaos and dramas . . . I created because of alcohol. . . . There was that hope that maybe I could feel this way again some day. And I didn't know why I wasn't feeling it out here. But there was always that link . . . that would draw me back to . . . 'this isn't right.' Because here I learned yes, no . . . . What is right and wrong and out there, I didn't have those boundaries and I didn't have that stability that dictates limits. . . . I didn't know how to [limit]. I did everything in excess.

"But back here, there was always . . . that comforting feeling and I always strove to try and find that. And I think to this day that's why I'm not in prison or that's why I didn't kill anybody. There was always somebody that saw good in me, because I was here and I had this good. . . .

Most of the time I was a very honest drunk, I was a very honest thief, I was a very honest liar," May chuckles. "That sounds contradictory but what it means is this piece of me was always with me, but I didn't know how to recognize it."

"Is that what you felt when you were doing things for your mother's funeral?" I ask.

"Yes. That completion of, 'Yeah, this is what I'm supposed to do.' And I was able to, to feel ah . . . in touch."

"In touch? Have you felt that way at any other time besides your mom's funeral?"

"When my granddaughter was born I was in the delivery [room] and watched her being born and was able to be with [my daughter], and I felt that then. Because there's always that beginning. Even the time I lay my mother to rest. . . . All of a sudden I could feel new life in terms of . . . I was sober, and I wasn't going to get drunk that day. . . . And I was going to be okay. . . . That's what it was, that feeling of comfort and knowing I did all I could and I'd done it the way I was supposed to do it. And it felt complete."

May continues talking about memories of her grandmother: "I can smell the sage burning and I'm back there . . . I could smell the beeswax. I can see the oval rug that I sat on by her big, overstuffed chair. And she'd do beading and rubbing the wax on the thread and she'd be talking to me, telling me stories and I'd just sit there."

May responds to a quick memory about getting her grandmother tea. "And that saucer being so huge, with her cup. My mother showed it to me and it was a little tiny saucer, a little tiny thing," May laughs. "And I'd watch her pour the tea in the saucer and pour it back in the cup to cool it off. . . .

"My grandma was [going] blind . . . but when we'd go up to the mountain and spend the summer, she'd take me out and she was zipping around and she was walking everywhere and she'd go, 'Okay, Isha [granddaughter] there's some.' And I'd climb the tree and get this black moss to make coom, which is a pudding. . . . And she'd say, 'Well, bring it down, fill up the gunny sack.' Then we'd go back and she'd wash it and pick all the sticks out and rinse it and rinse it and boil it on the stove and it was pudding. And I'd put sugar in it and eat it and she'd always make that for me. . . . And watching when they went and got honey. And watching her when she'd go out and get the [dried] meat hanging outside. . . . It was just part of what she did. You learned a lot and it all comes back at some point. [For example,] I didn't know how to butcher. One day my son, my oldest boy, brought in a half an elk. There I am, zip, zip. I had watched it somewhere in my life and it just all came back.

"For so many years it's been so clouded and so fragmented . . . a big collage that there hasn't been a real picture that's formed that I can look at. . . and have all those images. . . that are clear enough . . . that I can make some kind of sense out of. I've always had to live at somebody else's beat of the drum and I've always had to live at somebody else's will.

"And . . . even at 52, 1 am coming from puberty to womanhood to know who I am inside, finally. Because all that alcohol fog is now lifting, and all of that despair and . . . all of that life that was ebbing out of me. The light that I have is still there . . . and I can see that there is worth in here now. And I don't always have to look to other people for validation, because my spirit is starting to come back.

"And as an Indian woman at 52, I'm an elder," May whispers. "And I need to look at who I am, because people come to me to be taught. . . What I'm saying is that the modeling that I do in my behavior in all areas, in my profession, in my social life, in all of those things, people see me. Especially on the reservation, they used to see this drunk May; now they see this sober May. . . . I can see my color now. I can stand up and be counted. . . . [I can] lead, and not always be on the fringe looking in. We're taking back our culture, we're taking back our traditions and they fit very well."

May concludes: "There was a lot of hope in watching my mother and grandmother when they [did beadwork]. I watched them interact with other people and saw the respect that was given to them. I know that I came from that same lineage and maybe I can achieve that, too."

● The Fourth Circle: Coming Home

Long ago, before I was four years old—when my family, like so many other young Laguna and Acoma families in the 50s relocated to Barstow, California, so my father could work for the railroad—I learned that everything had a spirit, that everything had a place, that everything was connected.

I was surrounded by many brown grandmas, women with lights in their eyes and busy, wrinkled hands. I remember fresh corn and melons from the fields, dried deer meat hanging on the barbed wire fences, deer stew dinners with green Jello for dessert, red chili and fresh tortillas, peaches drying in the sun, the smell of warmth coming from the old wood stove, and hot oatmeal with canned milk. I "helped" my grandpa butcher sheep and chop wood, and helped my grandma rescue brown mountain bread from the hot outdoor ovens. I remember the excitement of preparations for welcoming the deer that the hunters would bring; the peacefulness of my grandpa praying out by the woodpile at sunrise; the sound of the village crier giving instructions and calling out news; and nights so full of stars my grandma got tired of counting them for me.

"Grandma, count the stars for me."

"There are too many to count, Gya-oh [A Laguna word meaning both grandmother and granddaughter]."

"How many are there?"

"More than a hundred, hundreds and hundreds. . . ."

"Grandma, what's a hundred?"

On some nights when my grandma was not too tired, she actually counted to a hundred for me. Some nights we both fell asleep before we got halfway there. She would start . . . 1, 2, 3. . . . We slept back to back and I could feel her breathing, her counting vibrating through that permeable spirit membrane that was me and her . . . 28, 29, 30. . . . We slept in the room that served as living room and bedroom in my grandma and grandpa's pueblo house in Paguate village. The room was warmed by a large wood stove that glowed with a red-orange light in a darkness that was cold on the edges; the kind of cold that made you pull your head under the covers in the early morning when the fire had long cooled . . . 53, 54, 55. . . . I'd watch the shadows swallow the fading light in the stove. My grandma's voice would fade with the light, drowsy . . . 72, 73. . . . Grandma! Are you still awake? . . . My grandpa would stir in his bed across the room and mutter, "Ah-ya-ah!" The counting would gain new strength. . . and soon, 88, 89 . . . 90. I knew 90. This was my signal to pull my pillow closer, to enjoy the full warmth of my grandma's body, to draw in the smell of pinon wood embers, to close my eyes and to sleep . . . 98, 99,100.

● Mother

"My mother . . . was really excited when Linda was born and so she did a lot of . . . buying clothes and [baby] Pendleton blankets . . . and always giving me money . . . for the baby. . . . And then she really loves Linda, because Linda was full-blood. And that's something that a lot of tribal elders hold in high regard, that someone be full-blood. And Linda is probably the closest to full-blood 'cause I have like white, German, and French in me."

May sighs and talks about the relationship with her mother. "We got along by talking and she might need to go somewhere and she'd come by and use the car. John [her husband] would drive it. And a lot of times if there was a funeral, I'd take her and we'd visit and she'd tell me stories about when she was young and how she was a jockey and we just talked and visited and laughed. She'd always come by when my daughter was like . . . 8 or 9 . . . and take her up and dig roots and taught her how to clean roots. And then we'd go up and pick huckleberries. . . .

And she never, ever said anything about my drinking. She'd just see I was drinking and she'd say, 'Well, I've got to go now. I just came by to see how you were and how the kids were.' And she'd always bring lots of food to the house. . . . And when I got [my first] house I was able to invite her to spend the night every once in a while. And I would get up early to make her oatmeal and get her 7-Up and all that stuff, and have it there for her when she woke up. And so she always enjoyed those things but there was never any touching. We never hugged. We never said, 'Hello'—a greeting or anything. She'd come in and we'd start visiting."

"How would you describe your relationship with her?" I ask.

"Well, I think we were more . . . real good acquaintances," May chuckles. "I think we were friends. Toward the end there, she was really trusting that I wouldn't drink and then she started having these strokes. Then she deteriorated until she didn't know who we were. And she thought my [granddaughter] Stacey who was probably about 11 months was [my daughter] Linda. We went to see mom at the nursing home and mom said, 'Oh Linda. You're so cute.'

"One of the things we never did do was touch. I kissed her just before she died. My children, they were in there when she was dying and they kissed her. They always had a good relationship with her."

"A touching relationship with her?"

"Yeah. She'd kiss them good night when she was at our house or if they were [at her house] because they were very insistent, you know. 'You will kiss me and that's it.' And so she would, and she'd always seemed a little surprised, you know every time they would do that. They'd just look at her husband John and nod and he'd go, 'Ya. Good night.'"

"How did you feel about her when she died?" I probe.

"I felt that we had really reached an understanding. I think I finally understood what she'd gone through with her alcohol. And that she understood my alcohol. And that I was sober now, and I had a feeling that she felt that I'd never drink again. I mean it was sort of in the present, and I don't know how to explain it, but it was sort of there. And so she'd come by and she'd hand me money to get something 'cause she knew that it wouldn't go for [drinking]. . . . So the trust was getting better. And I cared about her a lot. I'm sure love is proba-bly the word to describe that, but I'm still not sure how to separate all that feeling out, in terms of talking to my mother and about my mother."

"Is there still some . . . anger toward her or. . ." my question fades.

"Well it's not anger necessarily anymore. It's just the UNKNOWN. I don't know all the details and nobody ever told me all of them, or if they did, they were all one-sided and I never got to hear her side. And we never talked about it. It was nothing we ever talked about. We never talked about her drinking. We never talked about any of that. "What she talked about to me was when I was little and how my uncle was really proud that I could write my name at a very young age. One thing she did was to save all my little dishes that I used to play with. They were that amber glass, and it wasn't necessarily amber colored. There would be blues but it would be that really thick [glass], different cups and glasses that I had. And she saved them all and I got them when I was 22 years old. So she saved stuff for me.

"I haven't done that for my kids. I had a trunk with my kid's stuff in it but my ex-partner won't let me have them back. I have my son's vest, his buckskin and beaded vest and when he was a little tiny guy and my daughters [traditional] fan up here so. . ." May sighs.

"You said that you and your mother hadn't touched and you said the same thing about your father. . ."

"Uh-huh," says May.

"Were you expressive with your children?"

"Quite a bit when they were very small. Older, we didn't do that much. Now, when we see each other we kiss and when we kiss, we hug. I was very demonstrative to my grand-daughter. Her and I were [close] . . . before her father's family took her, before she was taken away.

After two troubled years of adolescence, May's first contact with other Indian people since being taken from her family would be in

Kansas at Haskell Institute, an all-Indian boarding school, when she was 17. Here, she trained in dining room management and learned to dance. She discovered that the dating interests of young men left her confused and uncomfortable, while her crushes on two or three female classmates were accepted and far more satisfying. For almost two years, she felt acceptance.

And here, despite dormitory restrictions and drinking prohibitions, May also learned to drink every chance she got, and when she could get it, she drank it all. Her attraction to alcohol would be solidified before her senior year in high school was finished. Her first blackout would occur the first time she drank. She remembers her peers coaxing her to take that first drink of vodka, but she doesn't remember the basketball game they went to see. What she liked was the feeling she got when she drank.

"I thought I could do things better. I became a little more bold especially around the girls. . . . And so, I could maybe dance closer. . . . Because when I drank then I could do whatever I wanted to do and . . . say 'excuse me'. . . 'cause I was drinking. 'Cause nobody really got hostile about it . . . besides the girls that I picked weren't pushing me away.

She drank heavily to cloak her heterosexual encounters so she consciously wouldn't remember them; her drinking excused her rage and periodic drunken announcements that she was homosexual. Her binge drinking exposed her to rapes, fights, and illegal activity while psychologically shielding her from responsibility. She would drink through her pregnancies with her two children, a son and a daughter. Sometimes, she would place them with people she didn't know when she was drinking; she'd move from place to place, with her children in tow, while maintaining her addiction.

"And I'd find myself in situations that I couldn't figure out how I got there. And . . . the FBI was after me because I'd sold [liquor] to an agent [on the reservation] . . . because we were wards of the federal government, so the FBI was involved. They were looking for me and they couldn't find me. I didn't have to go to jail [because] the time had run out. Those are really tough times to remember. It was, it was so mixed up. And so much alcohol . . . because I didn't want to feel any of it or deal with any of it."

May made three attempts to quit drinking: 28-day inpatient treatment programs at ages 34 and 35—this followed by 18 months of sobriety and a relapse—and again at 40. May quit drinking three months before her first granddaughter was born and two years before her mother died. AA meetings were the "drug" she substituted for alcohol.

She would attend meetings seven days a week, sometimes twice a day, and she opened the doors for a women's AA meeting in her Yakama community. Her two children complained that they saw more of her when she was drinking than during her first year of sobriety. It was clear that she could be excessive in other things.

"Had you observed other funerals so that you had an idea of what [was to be done]?" I ask.

"I had been to dressing services, but some of them were different in terms of, . . . the family was involved in dressing. And in our family, it wasn't the thing you did. You didn't go in and dress your family. You had somebody else do that. Others would cook; we were not to cook. We were not to handle the food because we were contaminated by death. I was able to sort that out and I had not a concept of it before. All of a sudden my role changed. Because everybody was talking to me about what needed to be done. . . .

"And people were saying that I didn't get drunk because my mother died." May stops and sighs as she remembers her uncle's funeral several years before. "I forgot all about Uncle Jimmy. I went to his funeral and stayed for the give-away, but I didn't stay any later than the beginning of the give-away because I wanted to go get drunk. . . . That was my mom's brother.

"And we have lessons that are always there," May continues. "It's just amazing, that stuff, and it's very natural. I always remember my grandma's altar. I always remember my mother's altar. And that's why I have an altar. I am not a bonafide, died-in-the-wool Shaker [Northwest Coast Indian religion] because I haven't been baptized or any of that. But I'm very much in the belief of what she did and I honor that. And the cross there," May points to a small alter, "the little gold cross is my mother's. They blessed it and they gave it to me the day of her funeral. The white cross behind it is when we blessed the house. The Shakers, one of the men who was officiating, made the cross for me . . . it's out of cedar, and he painted it, and that's where I put it, so. . . . I don't know why I have that up there other than . . . that's where it's supposed to be," May says. "And I tell people, 'Well, that's what's supposed to happen.' And they just go, 'Ri-i-i-ght. Talkin' that AA talk.' Well, that might be so, but the other part of it is the Native American, I know when things happen."

May talks about her color in relationship to her growth. As a child, she responded by washing vigorously when her classmates called her "nigger" or told her she was dirty because of the color of her skin. When she was a 9th grader, boys in the physical education class refused to dance with her because of her skin color. And when she had five years of sobriety, the doctors and staff at a local hospital assumed she was an alcoholic and put off treating her until she required emergency surgery for gall bladder problems. "I was Indian, wasn't I?"

In response to racism, May tries a balanced view. "White people can't understand racism because they don't wear skin color for a lifetime," she asserts. "I can't always spend all of my time educating people about who I am. I'm learning about me right now. But I am very fortunate in being able to do some workshops and things for people. It just sort of offends me when people presume they can tell someone else about me, because they don't know me.

Every phrase, every hesitation, every accent I use in my description is mine. It can't be anybody else. They haven't experienced that. That's what I mean about color. . . . How do I wear my color?

"I have found a place that I can call my own. . . . Belonging is being accepting of me and knowing that I'm okay. And I don't have to be anything more than that for anybody. As long as I can deal with May on a daily kind of voyage, then that's all I have to do. I don't have to be out there for anybody else in terms of 'let me rescue the world.' But I can be there as a teacher and a leader [by] just being who I am and letting people know that alcohol does kill. I've lived through it and I can walk on and talk about it and let people know that there is, there is a way out. And it doesn't have to be. . . a total, devastating, out-of-the-reach kind of hope. . . ."

● Reflective Inquiry

1. Do you believe it is essential that the researcher/interviewer be able to spiritually bond with the interviewee; and is it important that they share similar historical experiences? Explain. What are the implications of your answer for the profession.

2. What meaning does May's story have for you?

Healer/Healee, My Journey

By Arthur Soissons-Segal

This is a story of the author's healing journey from seeing himself as one with a disability to a whole person with ability. He reviews lessons he has learned and mutual healing interactions with persons who present psychotic disabilities.

started my healing journey in 1945 at the age of 14 while recovering from surgery for a cerebellar tumor. It was the start of a personal battle to find peace of mind, confidence, and connection. For years following the surgery, I struggled with poor coordination, inability to compete athletically and awkward social skills. I was lonely, isolated and insecure, longing for friendship and self-confidence.

In 1952 I was a student at the New York School of Social Work of Columbia University in group work, where we were taught to help people find ways to improve their quality of life. I now realize that my choice to work in the field of disability was an attempt to heal myself.

● A Budding Awareness

My second-year field work placement was at Blythedale, a residential rehabilitation center for children with physical disabilities. Hy Weiner, a beautiful and sensitive man, was my supervisor. Hy had a disability— petit mal epilepsy. His gentleness, self-assurance and sense of power

struck me; he did not present himself
as disabled. I wondered if only I
saw his epilepsy as a disability.

This was an early dawn-
ing of awareness, enhanced
by the children at the
Blythedale. Although con-
fined to bed, they played
softball hobbling around the
bases on crutches. The children experienced their abilities, not their disabilities, and
their self-confidence was enhanced
by staff praise

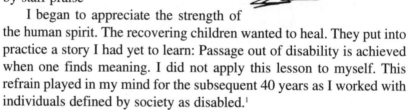

I began to appreciate the strength of
the human spirit. The recovering children wanted to heal. They put into
practice a story I had yet to learn: Passage out of disability is achieved
when one finds meaning. I did not apply this lesson to myself. This
refrain played in my mind for the subsequent 40 years as I worked with
individuals defined by society as disabled.[1]

I then learned about healing from Stanley Krippner at Saybrook
Institute, and the writings of Frankl (1978), Moustakas (1972), Cousins
(1979), and Siegel (1986) that emphasized the psychological and spiritual components of healing. I became aware of how laughter, self-
belief, and determination influenced healing. I read autobiographies
that described productivity and meaningfulness despite disabilities.
(Beisser, 1988; Brown, 1954; Hamshire, 1982; and Nolan, 1987). I
found support in knowing that individuals experience efficacy despite
their limitations. I learned that people find meaning in themselves
when open to wholeness. I began to see how the persons with disabilities seek to participate in "normal" activities of work and relationships.
I marveled when many of my clients denied that their disabilities prevented them from achieving independent living goals. They told me
that their motivation to recover was a major contributor to their ability
to feel good about themselves. I helped others reveal and experience

---

[1]At The Jewish Guild for the Blind, United Cerebral Palsy, the Institute for the Crip-
pled and Disabled (now the Howard Rusk Institute), Aid to Retarded Citizens (now The
ARC), and Community Mental Health.

their abilities. I helped social work students develop sensitivity to people with disabilities.

● Understanding My Own Blocks to Healing

Although clients and colleagues praised me, I could not respond to their accolades or acknowledge my strengths. I looked in the mirror and saw only blemishes and frailty. Acceptance of my limitations was so difficult to achieve. Society seeks perfection in us, and frailty is disparaged. To escape society's stigma, I denied my limitations which were so obvious to others.

I recall a farewell party honoring my work in organizing a developmental disability council into an effective advocacy group. The room filled with friends and fellow staff praised me and wished me well. After some especially flattering statement, embarrassed. I said, "Oh anyone could have done that," to which the speaker said, "Shut up and take credit for what you've done." My friend recognized my inability to accept praise. I was unaware then that this was a symptom of a disability that had a name, and that others with this disability had successful professional and personal lives. They could experience the pleasures of their success.

That knowledge was to come five years later. At the moment of the farewell party, the comment was received, laughed about, and forgotten.

● A Turning Point—Belonging And Normalizing

Several years later my work brought me into contact with colleagues who had learning disabilities (LD). This is sometimes subtle disability with a neurological origin that results in frustration and doubt about one's own abilities.

I worked with the LD agency, "The Puzzle People," for about a year when the executive director, a woman with LD, approached me and commented, "Art, you are one of us, you know." Her comments were calm and friendly.

I was relieved. My clumsiness and poor language skills had a name. My difficulty concentrating and tendency to move from one subject to another was comprehensible. I looked around. I knew these were me, or I was them. We had learning disabilities, dyslexia, attention deficit disorder. More importantly, we had each other. My symptoms had a name, and I had a support system.

Until that "Puzzle People" party, I blamed my poor coordination, reading problems, lack of concentration and other difficulties on my childhood brain tumor. The effect of that reasoning was as a rehabilitated brain tumor victim, I was alone without peers or role models. On the other hand, having LD brought peers, role models, and support. My humanness was validated. It was okay to be different. We could achieve our goals despite limitations.

Healing has been a continuing process of self-discovery. I had observed clients and colleagues risk self-disclosure. Finally I absorbed their self-descriptions and realized the match with my own. My readings, research and work experiences came together into a new healing pattern of self-awareness and acceptance.

● Healing

I see healing as letting go of pain to achieve health. It is a mending of one's spirit, pulling together body and soul, and accepting wholeness of self so as to experience meaningfulness.

Healing is a rebirth of the psychological self that somehow became lost in my developmental process. I began to develop comfort with my limitations, I "normalized" them. I felt part of a mainstream group of people with similar disabilities, and "that was okay."

● Experiencing (Rather Than Only Knowing) One's Abilities

There is a vast distance between an intellectual understanding of one's abilities and the experience of one's abilities. Intellectually, I acknowledged my achievements but did not own them.

An experience is an emotional internal event in that it is a feeling which one neurologically compares to prior feelings provoked by similar events. Thus, an experience is an emotion which absorbs itself in one's history. I believe that experience has the power to support or refute prior experiences, as my current experiences with success have refuted my historical experiences with limitation.

● New Healing In My Work

Normalization is a key component in my work with psychiatrically disabled adults. Currently, I coordinate a psychosocial rehabilitation service at the Hollywood Mental Health Center in Los Angeles. I help individuals to refer to themselves as people rather than as clients. We build upon strengths and plant seeds to produce more positive self-images. As they participate, many of them blossom and their social talk becomes lively. Many return to skills long in disuse. Some return to school; others venture out to employment. We help them to experience their abilities, neutralize their disabilities and feel connected to others. I believe that this sense of belonging is as healing for them as it has been for me. I respond to their experience of disability with calmness and a sense of, "So what's so terrible, we all have moments of that experience." Healing is an interactive experience. As I help them heal their wounds, I too heal.

● The Healer's Role

The healer's role, as I see it, is to present a self which invites the other person to reveal a desire to be healed. Just as I learned that disability, as well as ability, is a creation of the mind, we suggest to our clients that they have the power to create the self they want to be. Throughout the healing process, we seek out the positive attributes that we and they possess. We acknowledge the pain of their limitations but we dwell on their abilities. People share their successes. Together we celebrate happy occasions and discuss solutions to our problems. We benefit from the experiences of working together and helping each other. All of this builds a support system and a feeling of belongingness.

The healing process takes its own time. It cannot be hastened. It may be slow and take detours. Recovery is a lifelong process. Embarking on this journey requires a vision that wellness is attainable.

Like most wilderness trails, a healing path

twists steeply up zigzags, traverses narrow crevices, tumbles down inclines, and moves toward discovery. My clients and I pause to rest and experience the joy and excitement of the discovery.

For those who travel without guides, the healing points frequently go unnoticed until the big "WOW": the moment when the fog lifts and the trail brightens, the moment when the traveler commits to the work. For me, the "WOW" experience was the LD party.

The trail continues to the present rest stop, this chapter.

● References

Beisser, A. (1988). *Flying without wings: Personal reflections on loss, disability and healing.* NY. Bantam.

Brown, C. (1954). *My left foot.* London: Mandarin House.

Cousins, N. (1979). *Anatomy of an illness as perceived by the patient: Reflections on healing and regeneration.* NY. Bantam Books.

Frankl, V.E. (1978). *The unheard cry for meaning.* NY: Pocket Books.

Hamshire, S. (1982). *Susan's story: An autobiographical account of my struggle with dyslexia.* NY: St. Martins Press.

Moustakas, C.E. (1978). *Loneliness and love.* Englewood Cliffs, NJ: Prentice Hall.

Nolan, C. (1987). *Under the eye of the clock: The life story of Christopher Nolan.* NY: St. Martins Press.

Siegel, B.S. (1986). *Love, Medicine & Miracles: Lessons learned about self-healing from a surgeon's experience with exceptional patients.* NY: Harper & Row.

● Reflective Inquiry

1. Compare the similarities and differences of your experiences as a social work student/practitioner with those of the author, and account for them in the context of your view of spirituality.

2. What was the importance of feedback in introducing a change process in the author's life? Under what conditions do you find feedback helpful?

Meditation as a Tool That Links the Personal and the Professional

by Sadye L. Logan

This narrative explores the author's experience in using meditation to link personal and professional self in teaching, in relationships and toward self. I found as the practice of meditation progressed, my life took on new significance and meaning.

> *I shall be telling this with a sigh Somewhere ages and ages hence;*
> *Two roads diverged in a wood, and I, I took the one less traveled by —*
> *And that has made all the difference.*
>
> — *Robert Frost*

We are all seekers of truth on an extraordinary journey through life. Although I believe that the journey is essentially the same for everyone, there are some differences. These exist in our experience of the journey. This narrative is about the profound effects of meditation on my personal, professional and spiritual development.

The quote above from the poem by Robert Frost, "The Road Not Taken," captures the essence of this journey for me. Along the way I found I needed to answer these questions: Who am I? Where have I come from? Where am I going? How will I get there?

These questions are not reflective of queries specifically about my personal or professional endeavors, but are of a spiritual nature. Authors who address the subject of spiritual development tend to describe this questioning process as spiritual awakening or unfolding (Harris, 1989; Small, 1995). Unfolding has sometimes been described as slow and resistant, as gradual and welcoming, or as abrupt and tumultuous. Great seekers throughout the ages have referred to this process as coming out of sleep or a dream and coming alive or awakening to our true nature, to our essence (Muktananda, 1994; Fox, 1980; Ochs, 1983).

Although this unfolding happens in its own time from within, I have experienced this unfolding throughout my life. The subtleties of these experiences have not always been easy to discern. For the most part, they are powerful transitions or remembered events that somehow rearrange my usual or predominant ways of perceiving or being in the world. I define these transition points as life-changing events. In some instances these events are experienced as a personal crises that occur both naturally and unexpectedly (Lindermann, 1965; Ell, 1995). Generally, these natural events include going away to school, falling in love, getting married, learning to walk and talk, learning to play an instrument, having a mystical experience, or experiencing adolescence. Unexpected events include chronic or acute illnesses, divorce, tragic death, or an accident (Lindermann, 1965). Often those events and the more esoteric types of life-changing events are minimized as unimportant. For example, it's not unusual to read or hear stories similar to the ones below dismissed as esoteric or an unexplained passing event:

I wouldn't say that I am a deeply religious or spiritual person, but I do believe in a higher power. I have had some low moments in my life. They have been times when I have thought about dying, even about suicide. I can remember one day, however, walking along on a beautiful beach and feeling really depressed. I started wondering whether this higher power really exists. A strange thing happened. From somewhere inside of me, I heard a voice that said, "I am always with you."

I was walking alone in the woods one spring day when suddenly I started having this extraordinary experience—all of the trees and bushes around me were shimmering with a kind of radiant energy. It was as if they were alive in a special way—this energy was emanating from the trees and touching me. As they touched me, I seemed to meld with the trees and the energy. It was as if I were not different or separate from anything around me. Finally, this level of perceiving ended, but as I left the woods, I was tingling all over and felt great joy and happiness. This feeling stayed with me for weeks.

Some of my friends think it's a "little strange" that I view meditation and chanting as my form of worship. Some colleagues think that I am a "little strange" because I acknowledge spirituality as an important aspect of growth and development, and meditation as an important tool for self-growth and understanding. As a result of potential misunderstanding, I am careful how and to whom I speak about meditation. Further, I am finding it easier to be laughed at, albeit good humoredly, by colleagues, friends and others.

● Beginning of the Journey

The popular television actress Suzanne Sommers (1988) described an experience similar to those described above, which led to the writing of her book, *Keeping Secrets*. Sommers spoke of sitting for some time on a beautiful grassy ledge. Afterward she went indoors and began writing a book about growing up in an alcoholic family. She described writing the book as if it were being done by someone else. Recalling this event during a brief radio clip, "I think," she said, "something happened to me sitting on that ledge."

Unfortunately such stories often are dismissed as passing events of little or no importance. They are rarely viewed or experienced as an important point in the process of one's spiritual unfolding—a movement toward reconnecting with one's true essence. For me, moving into this awareness of my true nature, my essence, was like coming home to something that was so familiar. At the same time there was an elusive quality of something long forgotten. Meditation has served as an essential tool in propelling my process of reconnecting and remembering that which I already know: That I am a divine, perfected being.

I believe that this special journey begins with birth. For me, that beginning originated as a Gullah-speaking native on a Carolina sea island. Although I have come to view this culturally rich beginning as the perfect place to be born and raised, I didn't always feel that way. Initially, public opinion and negative sentiments about Gullah and Gullah-speaking people engendered shame, self-doubt and feelings of inferiority. My childhood on this beautiful, lush island was simple and joyful. A contrasting experience existed for adult islanders. Due in part to the harsh reality of segregation practices, poverty and lack of available jobs, life was a struggle. I was the eighth child in a family of seven brothers and two sisters. We grew up as Methodists in a religious family. As children, we attended Sunday schools, Sunday services and summer Bible school.

Growing up in the 1950s and the 1960s was an interesting, exciting time of bobby sox, crinoline slips, the Platters, sit-ins and protest demonstrations. Although I danced the twist and did the jerk and most of the things done by the youth of the time, there was a deeply serious side to me. An example of my serious side is that I believed in God—in a higher power—though I questioned the concept of a God of the fire and brimstone variety. My early ideas about God and religion came from my mother, lovingly called Claudia—my teacher and friend. She attempted to answer my questions about life in general and more specifically about who God is. Later questions were more spiritually oriented, and of the "who am I, and where am I going" variety.

In junior high I had the desire to know more about God, and committed myself to a more religious life by becoming an official member of the church family in which I grew up. I remembered stories that my mother told me about the older church members who sought their God in the traditional Gullah fashion. This consisted of the seeker initially experiencing an "inner calling" to know and serve God. When this "inner calling" was "heard," the seeker approached one of the church elders to guide him/her through a process called seeking. The seeker observes silence and becomes focused inward. He/she spoke to the elder and to others only when absolutely necessary. The elder interpreted dreams or visions and provided spiritual guidance to the seeker. The seeking period extended from three to six weeks. At the conclusion, the elder pronounced that the seeker had achieved the prerequisite experience to confirm full membership into the church family. The new member continued to grow and develop spiritually under the elder's guidance. The practice ended with my mother's generation and was no longer required in the church for full membership.

I loved this story and wanted this, or a similar experience of confirmation and God, in my life. This desire became a real issue for me during high school. I felt that if I did not experience God in this tangible form before leaving high school and the protection and guidance of my parents' home, I would never again seriously contemplate the concept of God or any of the life-transforming questions.

At first I attempted to force this process when I was in junior high school. I wanted to make it happen. This produced my first learning about spiritual awakening: It is not forced; it happens in its own time. Eventually I experienced a religious conversion. It began at an Easter sunrise service when I was a junior in high school. It led me to seek the guidance of Elder Crawford, a wise, thoughtful gentleman in our church. He provided me an experience of seeking God very similar to that of my great-great-grandparents. We met on a weekly basis and spoke about my dreams, thoughts and questions. Based on Elder Crawford's recommendation, I was accepted into full church membership. Even though my journey has taken me quite a distance from where I began, I still hold Elder Crawford as one of my most important guides. Reflecting over my life, I have come to view this experience as a significant catalyst for my current spiritual development.

My seeking, though, did not end with this confirmation experience in the mid 1960s. I explored several church organizations in the late 1970s—Baptist, Episcopalian and Unity—still searching for that irrefutable experience of God. As my questioning about who I am and where I was going became more intense, I began reading numerous spiritually oriented books, attended workshops, presentations and conferences. I was searching for something greater than a mundane experience. I wanted to know more about my overall existence about my higher self or God, and about how this higher self connects to my overall existence.

In the late 1970s, reading *Play of Consciousness or Chitshakti Vilas,* the spiritual autobiography of Swami Muktananda Paramahamsa, one of the great spiritual masters of our time, marked another transition for me. His yoga is called Siddha Yoga, the perfect path, the path of love. This book propelled my journey in an unexpected direction. Muktananda's teaching is simple, universal and profound: God dwells within you as you for you. In other words, within every human being divinity exists. Spiritual practice is not separate from everyday existence, but a part of it.

● The Awakening

I did not begin the practice of meditation until 1982, when I met a great spiritual master and teacher, Swami Chivilasananda, the current head of the lineage of Siddha Yoga Masters entrusted with the lineage when Her spiritual teacher (Guru) Swami Muktananda died in 1982. 1 have meditated under Her guidance since 1982. She is a Siddha Guru and has the power and knowledge to give others the inner experience of God, and is dedicated to sharing that experience. She awakens a seeker's spiritual energy through Shaktipat initiation. From that time on She offers seekers guidance along the spiritual path to complete self-realization. Over the past 13 years, I have spent time in Her presence in the West as well as the East. Free of all limiting qualities, She exudes a presence of pure unconditional love. She lives in a state of total awareness. Chivilasananda continues the Guru's tradition, offering the teaching of the Siddhas and Shaktipat initiation to seekers around the world.

As my meditation progressed and I practiced more regularly and consistently, my life took on new significance and meaning. In the beginning, my understanding of meditation and its benefits was somewhat unbaked, to put it mildly. On some level I expected to sit a few times and have all the profound experiences that I had read or heard others talk about. It didn't work that way. I have come to know and respect my meditation practices as a personal journey that unfolds according to my spiritual needs and self-effort. I have come to recognize that the outcome is a subtle process reflected in my ways of seeing and being in the world.

Initially I witnessed my inner transformation through meditation in the form of behavioral changes. For example, old habits of subtly putting myself down and limiting impressions seemed to simply vanish. These "old tapes" were about not being smart enough, pretty enough or articulate enough or about experiences that made me feel contracted. I found myself becoming centered in an inner place of calmness and clarity. The fear that accompanied the limiting impressions was gradually dissipating. A useful image of this process is a huge iceberg, with a crack straight through the center, being moved out to sea and melting slowly by the warming effects of the ocean air. The iceberg is the limiting impressions eroded by the meditation process represented by the warming effects of the ocean air. These are all the signs that a powerful meditative energy has been released—dynamically and spontaneously. Those old self-defeating ideas were being peeled away like layers of an onion. My perception is confirmed by friends, family and colleagues who say things to me such as, "We see such confidence in you" and "There's a kind of peace or calmness in your presence."

I recall several occasions when visiting my former social work practicum instructor, Ruth Brenner, from Hunter College School of Social Work in New York City. Ruth would always marvel at how much I had changed, and inevitably ask: "Are you in therapy?" Somehow my response about meditation was never acknowledged. I assumed that she could not accept that meditation provided such results. Friends and colleagues responded in a similar manner. Some were curious, others changed the subject, and a rare few asked for instruction or more information. These responses are not unusual in that most people believe that meditation is exotic and done by those who might be just a little strange.

Daily practice of meditation allows me to live my life fully and present in every moment. To me, this means to practice living in the awareness that a divine consciousness exists within me as me, for me, and that same consciousness exists within fellow human beings, all other creatures, as well as every particle of the universe. Although this view of my existence may sound somewhat radical, it is an awareness that puts a different slant on the way I live my life daily. Problems and concerns are placed in a calm, manageable perspective. I often describe this way of being as similar to living in the "eye of the hurricane." Regardless of what exists around me, centered within myself I am responding calmly and undisturbed.

Problems are more obvious during stressful situations. When my car rolled into the street, it was totaled by a passing dumpster truck. The truck driver said how sorry he was while I stood there feeling as if I had just lost a close relative. I struggled with numerous emotions, especially anger at the truck driver. Recognizing what was happening, I choose to focus inside and watch my breath. Soon I became calm and inwardly forgave the truck driver instead of wanting to blame him. I have experienced similar situations on more than one occasion with groups of angry students.

I teach a year-long foundation practicum course. It is one of the most challenging, yet invigorating courses in the curriculum. Due to the students' diversity in terms of level of preparedness, expectations and experiences, many students come into the program with a great deal of anxiety and assumptions about how the course should be taught. There is an ongoing challenge in working toward achieving a balance between discussion about practicum matters and teaching content that requires students to think, write and speak critically about their practice.

It goes without saying that such situations are fertile ground for misunderstanding and conflict. There was a group of four students in a class of 16 who, through fidgety behavior, little or no overt participation in class discussion, and a general air of dissatisfaction with the class. I engaged the entire class in dialogue about what appeared to be apathy. This discussion dissipated the uneasiness and lowered the anxiety.

Later in the semester I read a student paper to the class to illustrate a practice principle. Carey, a student who acted as the spokesperson for the class, spoke out in a hostile, attacking tone, suggesting that I should have read the paper earlier in the semester to provide more detailed guidelines about what I wanted in papers. Carey's criticism sparked the voices of the other three students. The remaining class members, even those who disagreed with Carey, became very quiet. In that moment I felt attacked and struggled not to react defensively. It would have been easy to attack back, but again, I choose to focus inside, breathe deeply and respond to the student's accusation instead of reacting out of frustration and anger. Soon the tension dissolved and the situation was dealt with in a calm, respectful manner. Students have come to view such situations as teachable moments. I view them as opportunities to model for the students as well as to practice what I am learning from my meditation practices.

● The Unfolding

As suggested earlier, it is evident that my interactions with family, friends and colleagues are being transformed, but more importantly, I have become more compassionate with myself. I have become softer and kinder to myself. I am tuning in less to old, self-defeating tapes that subtly undermine my confidence in my abilities. I take time to nurture myself, to spend time with friends, family and nature. I can now say "I love you" very easily to my loved ones. There is a lightness, a spontaneity, a joyfulness. In concert with such powerful, personal changes, I began speaking and teaching my social work classes from an understanding that transcended the mind, from an understanding of my heart. The lightness of being that I am experiencing daily spills over into my classroom in the form of openness, spontaneous role plays, more concrete and specific practice example. In short, my classroom lectures have became more personable, more alive, more natural. During the early period of my teaching career, there was often dissonance between what my students thought they wanted and what I thought they needed. Now I witness more enthusiasm in my students about the subject matter and more commitment to the work. They take more risks in bringing work to the classroom, engaging in the role plays, joining in open dialogues and critically analyzing practice-related issues and concerns. It seems to me that my students and I are growing to genuinely like and respect one another in different ways.

● The Journey Continues

It is obvious from the foregoing that I am excited about the potential of meditation as an integrative tool for personal and professional growth. I believe it is especially relevant in view of the turbulence which exists within us and in the world around us. Our world is filled with anxiety, violence and hatred. Although love and caring do exist, it is not nearly enough. It is important that we work more consistently to love ourselves and to strengthen our spiritual selves.

Muktananda (1985) reminds us of this. He states:

> *Everything we do in life we do in the hope of experiencing love. Love is essential for all of us. There is a sublime place inside us where love dwells. That is why we meditate. Through meditation the inner love is unfolded. As we constantly meditate we get drunk on this inner love and that is when we begin to realize what love really is.* (175–176)

Despite my excitement for the potential that meditation holds for clients as well as helpers, meditation is still a new venture for social work and other helping professions. I do not wish to give the impression that if one sits down to meditate sporadically that one would achieve the highest goal of meditation. I am suggesting though, that not unlike other practices, meditation requires consistency and continuity.

Further, it is important to recognize that from the point of treatment intervention, meditation gives meaning to a strength-based, solution-focused perspective. In other words, it enhances and reinforces life skills such as the ability to concentrate, discriminate, be present-centered. Overall mediation has removed my fear and feelings of inadequacy and supports me in living my life to its fullest.

● References

Fox, M. (1983). *Original blessing.* San Francisco: Bear and Company.
Harris, M. (1989). *Dance of the spirit.* New York: Bantam Books.

Lindermann, E. (1965). Symptomatology and management of active grief. In R. Fulton (Ed.), *Death and identity* (pp. 186–201). New York: John Wiley and Sons.

Ochs, C. (1983). *Women and spirituality.* Totowa, NH: Rowman and Allanfeld.

Sommers, S. (1988). *Keeping secrets.* California: Warner Press.

Swami Muktananda. (1994). *Play of consciousness,* 4th ed. New York: SYDA Foundation.

Swami Muktananda. (1985). *I am alive: Secrets of the inner journey.* New York: SYDA Foundation.

● Additional References

Anonymous Poem in Transformation: *On Tour With Gurumayi Chidvilasananda,* September 1986–September 1987, p. 60. New York: SYA Foundation.

Swami Durgananda. (1983). Forward. In Swami Mukananda (Ed.), *Where are you going? A guide to the spiritual journey* (pp. v–xii). Garespuri, India: Gurudev Siddhapeeth.

Swami Chidvilasananda. (1989). *Kindle my heart,* vols. I and II. New York: SYDA Foundation.

Swami Muktananda. (1983). *Where are you going: A guide to the spiritual journey.* Garespuri, Inida: Gurudev Siddhapeeth.

Swami Muktananda. (1986). *Kundalin: The secret of life.* Garespuri, India: Gurudev Siddhapeeth.

● Reflective Inquiry

1. The author notes that questions such as: Who am I? Where have I come from? Where am I going? How will I get there? are of a spiritual nature. How do you view this? Have these sorts of questions come up in your practice experience? Explain.

2. What is your view of meditation, and its relationship to how people interact? Would you use meditation in your practice? Explain.

3. Would you consider learning how to meditate? If not why not? and if yes, what do you consider the obstacles?

Spirituality in First Nations Storytelling: A Sahnish-Hidatsa Approach to Narrative

by Michael James Yellow Bird

In this narrative I share four aspects of storytelling that support the spirituality of First Nations' people. I begin with a Portion of the Sahnish genesis story and its identification of our spiritual beliefs and history. I discuss the significance and Purpose of traditional narratives in relation to the manner of storytelling by the elders in our village.

⬤ Sahnish-Hidatsa Narrative

Storytelling among First Nations people has a long and rich history. In my village, the oral traditions of my people remain one of the most important ways to define and give meaning to our Indigenous spirituality. Our stories teach us that spirituality is the knowledge of, value for, and participation in our sacred ceremonies and traditions. The telling of certain sacred and non-sacred stories and events by different members of our peoples often is intended to support and preserve our spirituality. For example, many of our narratives present circumstances, places, persons, or events that ensure that our people remember who we are, how we should behave, what we should know and value, and where we came from. Our stories help us to honor and respect the struggles and experiences of our ancestors and contemporaries and enable us to pass on our oral histories to our children and grandchildren.

In this chapter, I prefer not to use the words "Indian" or "Native American" to name my peoples. We are not from India. Also, the term "Native American" could refer to anyone who is born in the Americas. I prefer to be called Sahnish and Hidatsa, which are my Nations. I also prefer the terms First Nations, aboriginal, or indigenous to refer to my peoples collectively.

The purpose of this article is to share four different aspects that relate our people's storytelling to spirituality. To set the context, I begin with our Sahnish genesis story along with our spiritual beliefs and history. Then follows a discussion of the way storytelling helps to promote spiritual thinking and actions among our peoples. Next, I tell the way elders in my village share their personal narratives in a community setting as an example of a traditional form of storytelling. I then discuss the reasons the telling of the stories in our indigenous language is diminishing, illustrated by my mother's narrative about my Hidatsa grandfather's "Indian" boarding school experience.

The Sahnish-Hidatsa approach to narrative that I share throughout this chapter is based upon my own experiences and constructions and should not be construed as definitive. The Sahnish and Hidatsa are two different nations. Each has its own rich and wonderful stories, storytellers, and ideas of what stories mean and how they should be told. I hyphenate the two nations since I am a member of both groups.

● The Importance of our Genesis and History in Sahnish Narrative

Recounting our people's genesis and history is one of the most important examples of the way our oral traditions support our spirituality. Our people, like many other First Nations, believe that we have lived and moved throughout "Great Turtle Island" (the Americas) since time immemorial (Wright, 1993; Maracle, 1993). Our origin stories have always helped to create within our peoples a sense of belonging, purpose, and relatedness with all other forms of life. For eons, the genesis narratives of the Sahnish have taught us that we, along with all other living things, existed first in an embryo state deep within the womb of Mother Earth. As our desire to attain a higher state of perfection grew,

Neshanu Natchiktak (the supreme being of power and wisdom) and Mother Corn (the intermediary between humans and Neshanu Natchiktak) heard our cries, pitied us and helped us emerge from Mother Earth. Mother Corn gave us the gift of corn which gave us life and enabled us to live as human beings. She guided us on a long migration from the south to show us where to live. Our traditional narratives teach us that, as we developed into humans and journeyed to our destination, we endured many hardships and tragedies which often compelled us to call upon Mother Corn to intercede on our behalf. We are taught to have reverence and gratitude to Mother Corn for all she has done for us.

Our oral traditions also clearly point out that our emergence from Mother Earth occurred in this part of the world in the southern hemisphere. Indeed, none of our sacred bundles, which represent the most ancient memories of our people, tell us that we crossed the Bering Strait as anthropologists suggest.

Our peoples now live on the Fort Berthold reservation, located around the Upper Missouri river in North Dakota. I come from a small Sahnish village called White Shield, which was named after one of our most respected Chiefs. In our languages, Sahnish means "the people" while Hidatsa means "river or willow crow." My father is Sahnish and my mother is Sahnish and Hidatsa. My father's people are closely related to the Skidi Pawnee who once lived in Nebraska but now reside in Oklahoma. My mother's people, on her father's side, are closely related to the Crow Nation, which resides in southeastern Montana.

The Sahnish refer to the Missouri river as the "Mysterious or Holy River" since it was important to many of our most sacred ceremonies. Before 1953, we lived along the flood plain of this river and raised several varieties of corn, squash, and beans in the rich soils that were deposited there. We also grew potatoes, melons, pumpkins, sunflowers, and tobacco, all of which are indigenous to Great Turtle Island (Weatherford, 1991; Gilmore, 1987). The caretakers of our gardens were the women who engaged themselves in highly complex planting and harvesting rituals. In between these two seasons, they would clean and water the gardens and sing to the crops as if the crops were their own children. We often traded many of our crops with other indigenous people for horses, buffalo meat, robes and other things we may have needed.

I was not raised on our traditional homelands beside the holy river. The U.S. Army Corps of Engineers, despite our elder's protests that our lands were protected under the "Treaty Of Fort Laramie, made in 1851" (Meyer, 1977, p. 217), built the Garrison Dam just south of our reservation, which flooded out 155,000 acres of our richest lands. Our gardens, timber, sacred sites, and ancient way of life were inundated to control floods and produce electricity for people farther downstream whom we never even knew. We were relocated to higher, more barren grounds on our reservation and given welfare as a substitute for our sustainable way of life. I never saw the wonderful gardens of our people or experienced the traditional village ways. But my grandmother (White Eagle Woman), always said, "Oh, it was so beautiful there. You children just don't know how beautiful it was."

The Sahnish genesis story reminds us of our connections to the land, the sacred beings, and the ways of our ancestors. It also reminds us to protect and to honor our spirituality since it is often violated for the sake of other peoples' "progress" and "development."

● A Sahnish-Hidatsa Approach to Narrative

While personal narratives are told to assist the storyteller to process everyday experiences and events, they are also shared to help promote spiritual thinking and behavior in the village community. Many times narratives are told to help reaffirm our identity and to remind us of our purpose in life and in death. Since I am related to many people in my village, the stories usually tell me something about the emotional and spiritual state of our peoples. Narratives are told in order to teach our people about morality and to raise awareness and concern for one another. They help to instill in the individual and the village membership a passionate desire for both greatness and humility while stressing the importance of sacrifice, prayer, and courage. Narratives help to keep our indigenous spirituality alive by reminding us of our responsibilities in ancient rituals and ceremonies.

There are two aspects that I think are very important to a Sahnish-Hidatsa approach to narrative. The first aspect is a particular manner of the storytelling which is affected by the place where the story is told and the person telling the story. This manner is illustrated by the way our elders tell stories. The second aspect is the language in which the story is told. Traditionally, stories are conveyed orally and personally. The meanings are closely tied to the nuances of the particular spoken language. Unfortunately, storytelling in our indigenous languages continues to diminish at a steady rate. Many of the elders in our village, who in earlier times would have passed the languages on to us, are not fluent speakers because they attended federal government and religious mission schools where they were coerced to learn English. Although the children in our village spend some time learning our language in school, they spend significantly more time learning English. The use of English to tell our stories is problematic since it changes the tenor and manner in which a story is told. Many times there are no comparable words in English that can convey the intent and meaning of our languages. For me, the declining use of our languages to tell our stories further threatens the loss of our identity and contributes to our emotional and spiritual distress. This point will be conveyed through the story of my own grandfather.

● The Person to Village Narrative: Storytelling by the Elders

In many instances, the narrative among my peoples has not been an individual person-to-person event. In my village, one traditional approach occurs when an individual shares a narrative with several people at once. The best example of this is when our elders "stand up" during public gatherings or ceremonies and share their personal stories. Sometimes they are asked to "offer some words," while at other times their sharing is a spontaneous action. Depending upon the event, the narrative may be either very humorous and uplifting or very painful and sad. Sometimes it can admonish the listeners for the injustices, failures, and unnecessary complacency in the village. At other times, the stories are gentle, motivating, and inspiring and call upon the generosity and kindness of the people in the village to address a pressing issue.

There seems to be a predictable pattern in the process and delivery of this type of oral story. The speakers usually begin by explaining to the audience their hope that what they are about to share will help the people in some way. Then, they generally put forth a disclaimer that their knowledge is limited and apologize for taking this time to talk about themselves or share what they know.

I expect that most outsiders would think this type of opening means that the storyteller has a lack of confidence or poor public speaking skills. On the contrary, by opening this way, the elders are reminding us to "respect what you know," "remember you don't know everything," and "think for yourself." When I compare our elder's opening statements with those of other speakers who claim to be "the experts" but convey little, I now realize that my elders were really teaching me humility and intellectual freedom.

Following the opening, elders generally share one or more of their own meaningful experiences, especially those with special relevance to the occasion, the audience, and the request that has been made of them. During this time, many of their narratives convey some of their deepest emotions of grief, anger, humor, and delight. As I have listened to their stories, I have found that many of the things that they share are very emotionally and spiritually liberating. I find myself fully listening and reaching for the important messages that may be conveyed in the narrative.

Often their stories are quite lengthy and, at times, contain long pauses between different words and ideas. Sometimes certain words and phrases are said in our Sahnish language which I cannot understand. Many times I have turned to my mother or father and asked, "What did they say?" They generally do not look at me but usually answer with a slight frown and quick point at the speaker with their lips, which means "pay attention, something important is being said." I'm generally quiet after this directive.

As I reflect on my grade school experiences, I am reminded that our elders' style of narrative was clearly in conflict with how the local Bureau of Indian Affairs (BIA) school teachers expected us "Indian" kids to speak. They often pointed out to us that we needed a quick, to the point, "look at me when I am talking to you" kind of delivery. Learning this style of speaking made me impatient with our elderly storytellers. However, it also made me very nervous about what the government teachers would say whenever I would slip into the traditional style of narrative delivery at school.

One of the things I remember most about the traditional manner of storytelling is that, despite all of the time taken to tell the narrative and the indeterminacy of certain expressions, no one in the audience would ever interrupt or tell the person "we are running out of time so you have to hurry up," or "would you please define or explain what you mean?" As listeners, we were expected to develop patience and search for answers to the questions that were triggered by the person's narrative.

Each elder always had his or her own way of ending the narrative. Some would finish by adding a bit of humor to their story by telling a joke. Others would tell an amusing, unexpected story about themselves or someone else, which usually got a big belly laugh and "happy" tears from the audience. I believe that this ending is very important since one of the chief codes of our peoples is not to dwell too long in angry words or thoughts and not to leave in an angry way when speaking publicly.

When the storyteller is finished, he or she again thanks the audience members for their patience and time. The speaker often repeats the statement "I don't know that much" and apologizes for taking time to talk about him or herself. When the person sits down, members of the audience often seek out the storyteller and offer some tobacco, a blanket, some gas money, or a handshake to thank him or her for what was said for the benefit of the people. To me, this entire process reaffirms the importance of this type of narrative for creating a sense of spiritual well-being and connection. It also demonstrates the position of our elders as our most prominent storytellers.

● The Diminishing Sahnish Narrative: Policies of the "Great White Father"

Sharing a personal narrative in the traditional language has not always been possible. When First Nations peoples were "removed" to reservations, many indigenous children were federally mandated to attend government and religious missionary schools for "civilization" purposes. Our peoples were among those who had to participate in the "Great White Father's" (United States Commissioner of Indian Affairs) forced acculturation programs.

As a matter of public policy, which was usually directed by the Great White Father, these schools prevented First Nations children from using their indigenous languages and deliberately neglected any discussions that would allow the children to promote or understand their indigenous identities. For example, on July 16, 1887, J.D.C. Atkins, Commissioner of Indian Affairs, wrote the following to all schools that educated Native students:

Your attention is called to the regulation of this office which forbids instruction in schools in any Indian language. This rule applies to all schools on an Indian reservation, whether government or mission schools. The education of the Indians in the vernacular is not only of no use to them, but is detrimental to the cause of their education and civilization. You are instructed to see that this rule is rigidly enforced in all schools upon the reservation under your charge. No mission school will be permitted on the reservation which does not comply with the regulation. (Prucha, 1976, p. 175)

Two years later, another Commissioner of Indian Affairs, Thomas J. Morgan, issued a directive calling for the "Inculcation of Patriotism in Indian Schools" (Prucha, 1976, p. 180). In this order he states that:

In all proper ways, teachers in the Indian schools should endeavor to appeal to the highest elements of manhood and womanhood in their pupils . . . and they should carefully avoid any unnecessary reference to the fact that they are Indians. (Prucha, 1976, p.181)

The punishments were often very severe for children caught speaking their language or identifying with their people. Children as young as 4 and 5 years old who attended these schools (I call them forced acculturation camps) were tortured, abused, and ridiculed for speaking or acting like an "Indian." After these children returned to their homelands, grew to adulthood, and became elders, many refused to or could not teach their children or grandchildren their traditional language. I am certain that these years of colonialist imperialism and inculcation caused many of our peoples to be ashamed of who they are and contributed to the lack of interest in learning and teaching our languages.

My family's narrative of the "Indian" boarding school experience, similar to that of many other indigenous peoples, has a lot to do with surviving and trying to understand that experience (Haig-Brown, 1988; Knockwood, 1992). It is especially significant since it is the historical juncture where personal narratives in our own indigenous languages began to decline.

Over the years, my mother has shared with me my Hidatsa grandfather's personal story of his experiences in the "Indian" boarding school system. For me, it is one of the most profound and difficult stories to hear. Whenever I hear his narrative, I often go through many intense emotions—grief, anger, and fear to name only a few—and react with long, deep silences. As my mother tells me his story, she often begins by describing how my grandfather was taken from our reservation in North Dakota and sent to Hampton Institute in Virginia. She never forgets to tell me that most of his experiences there were very terrifying and lonely. He was one of the "Indian" children who didn't have a choice—he had to go! The "Indian agent" would go among the people and select different children they thought would benefit from being sent away. She says that he was "just a little boy when he went there, maybe 6 or 7 years old." What he remembered most about his experience was being severely beaten and punished many times. He said, "Sometimes they just used their fists, but other times they used a horse whip." The part of the narrative that she shares most often with me, however, has to do with his not being able to understand or speak English. "He could only speak Indian and didn't know what they were saying to him or what they wanted him to do, so they would beat him up," she says wiping her nose and eyes.

Whenever she tells me his story, her tears always well-up, and she never looks directly at me, which is unusual for such a loving mother. But my response is usually the same, so I rarely look at her when she tells me this part. She tells me that "many other bad things happened to him there." She suggests that maybe many of the difficult times that he experienced in his adult life had a lot to do with his beatings and cruel treatment at the "Indian" boarding school. Sometimes while she is telling me his story, my mind recalls the pictures I saw in a book about Hampton that showed the headstones on the graves of the little "Indian" children who died there. Being a parent, I often think of how heartbroken and shattered these children's moms and dads must have been when they learned of their children's death. Unable to hold their child for the last time or perform the proper burial ceremonies, they must have undergone tremendous shock and grief. I know as long as I live I will never forget these images in the stories my mother has told me.

I often think that my grandfather's narrative now belongs to my mother. While it is a horrible story, I know that she faithfully guards and shares it as a tribute to his surviving the "Indian" boarding school experience. I sometimes dream that when she is telling me his story, his spirit is rescued and lifted free from his terror and suffering for being an "Indian." And, although she has never said it, I am sure that she wishes she could have been there to cradle and protect this child from his "civilized" tormentors.

I am certain that the horrible and inhumane experiences suffered by First Nations children in these schools changed, forever, the meaning and sharing of the personal narrative of indigenous peoples. I know that my grandfather shared the Indian boarding school stories only with my mother when he was an elder in our community. He did not tell anyone what happened to him until he had been the tribal judge and served on the tribal council. I wondered why he waited so long to share his narrative. Maybe the reason is that he wanted his daughter (my mom) to avoid having to carry his pain and, thus, "giving" it to his grandchildren. Then he thought it was necessary to tell her these things when she became a mother and responsible for keeping her children safe. Or maybe he waited because, somewhere in his dreams, there still lingered a nightmare of Commissioner J.D.C. Atkins' "rigidly enforced" rule which brutalized indigenous children for speaking their languages or acting like an "Indian."

When my grandfather did share his personal narratives with my mother, they were not in our indigenous languages; they were in English. When my mother shared with me my grandfather's stories, they were also in English. And now I share these same narratives with my children in English. In 1887, Commissioner of Indian Affairs, J.D.C. Atkins, wrote, "No unity or community of feeling can be established among different peoples unless they are brought to speak the same language . . ." (Prucha, 1976, p. 175).

After considering this statement of the "Great White Father" on different occasions, I often wonder why, then, there have been many times that my grandfather, mother, and I, all English-speaking people, have never really felt like "Americans" or like a part of the American community. As I ponder the reasons for our feelings, I think maybe there have been too many John Wayne movies and too many John Wayne "wannabees." Maybe there have been too many presidents like George Bush who have said "I never apologize for the United States of America. I don't care what the facts are" (Wright, 1993, p. 212). Or maybe there have been too many Washington Redskins or Atlanta Braves games with too many tomahawk chops and too few protesters. I'm not sure. What I do know, however, is that, now, I rarely wonder why my English-speaking children's personal narratives contain many splinters of the same fears as my grandfather's mother's, and mine. Often, I wonder how long the "Great White Father's" "civilizing efforts" will haunt us.

On the one hand, my grandfather's "Indian" boarding school experiences are partly responsible for my family's inability to learn or speak our languages. Without our languages it is extremely difficult to teach and practice our spirituality or to share our most sacred traditional stories in appropriate and meaningful ways. On the other hand, his experience reminds me that our Sahnish genesis story teaches us that our lives have not been without difficult and tragic times, and maybe it is now time to call on Mother Corn.

● Summary

Storytelling in my village is one of the most important ways to define and give meaning to our spirituality. Our stories teach about our ceremonies and traditions which we should value and participate in. There are four different aspects of storytelling that help to point out the relationship between our people's narratives and spirituality.

1. The first is the perspective provided by our Sahnish genesis story, which helps to create a sense of purpose, belonging, and relatedness among our peoples and all other life. Indeed, telling our history reminds us of who we are, where we came from, and what we should expect from our future.

2. The second aspect is that personal narratives are often used to help individuals or the village membership to reaffirm their identity and purpose in life and death. They also tell us something about the emotional and spiritual state of our peoples and remind us of our responsibilities to one another and our traditions.

3. A third aspect is the manner in which our stories are told. An example of this aspect is the way in which our elders publicly share their personal narratives. This traditional approach teaches the village membership about humility, respect, and patience.

4. The fourth aspect relates to the impact of the policies of the "Great White Father" which censured the use of indigenous languages by indigenous children who were forced to attend federal government and religious boarding schools. As my grandfather's "Indian" boarding school experience illustrates, not only is there a loss of traditional language among First Nations peoples, but there are also many emotional and spiritual scars that remain.

The narratives in my village attest to the pain, loss, resiliency, hope, and humanity that are found among our peoples. Persons in the helping professions who are interested in indigenous narratives must understand that not all First Nations peoples are willing to share their personal stories in public gatherings or in private. It is important to remember that narratives will vary according to the traditions of each First Nations group. Most of all, it is important to listen carefully and honestly and to be sensitive and respectful to the storytelling protocol of each group.

● References

Gilmore, M. R. (1987). Prairie smoke. St. Paul: Minnesota Historical Society Press.

Hag-Brown, C. (1988). *Resistance and renewal: Surviving the indian residential school.* Vancouver: Tillacum Library.

Knockwood, I. (1992). *Out of the depths.* Lockeport, Nova Scotia: Roseway Publishing

Maracle, B. (1993). *Crazywater: Native voices on addiction and recovery.* Toronto, Ontario: Penguin Books Canada Ltd.

Meyer, R.W. (1977). *Village Indians of the Upper Missouri: The Mandans, Hidatsas, and Arikaras.* The University of Nebraska Press.

Prucha, F.P. (1975). *Documents of United States Indian Policy.* Lincoln: University of Nebraska Press.

Weatherford, J. (1991). *Native roots: How the Indians enriched America.* Ballantine Books.

Wright, R. (1993). *Stolen continents.* Toronto, Ontario: Penguin Books Canada Ltd.

● Reflective Inquiry

1. Dr. Yellow Bird explains that recounting "our people's genesis and history is one of the most important examples of the way our oral traditions support our spirituality?" What are some of the narratives in your background that support your spirituality?

2. Dr. Yellow Bird writes about naming. He notes that he prefers that the words "Indian, or Native American not be used to name "My peoples." His preference is to be referred to by his Nation, Sahanish and Hidatsa, which are his nations, or collectively "First Nations." What is your view of this form of identifying persons that are Aboriginal to the U.S.

3. He says the because of boarding schools and restrictions against using indigenous language, many First Nation's persons do not know their own aboriginal language. What experiences have you had in which language has been used for control?

Name Index

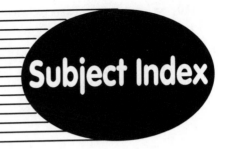

Subject Index

A

"Adult child" in Three-Child
    Model, 35, 36
African cultures, 54, 55-56, 57,
    58, 63
Al-Fataha, 8
Atkins, J.D.C., 119-120, 122

B

Bedouin-Arab
    family structure of, 7-8, 9
    guidelines for treating, 25
    people and culture, 5, 6-7, 13
    proverb, 14-15
Bethune, Mary McLeod, 63
Bilu, Y., 17
Black Power Movement, 52, 53
Black Studies, 53
Brenner, Ruth, 109
Bureau of Indian Affairs (BIA),
    118

C

Child welfare, recovery from,
    82, 84-85
Christian belief, 76

Clay, Charles, 47
Crosby, Michael, 37, 47
Civil rights movement, 53-54
Cultural
    pluralism, 54
    sensitivity, 5
Culture, black, 55.
        See also Kwanzaa

D

Dervishes, 8, 18, 19, 21, 22

F

Faith, 70
    rewards of, 78-80
Fanon, Frantz, 64
First Nations people and
        language, 113, 119, 121,
        123-124
Fort Berthold reservation, 115
Frost, Robert, 103

G

"Godhead" as third child state,
    35